The Tempting of Audra Grey

The Tempting of Audra Grey

Tricia Padgett

Pacific Press Publishing Association
Boise, Idaho
Oshawa, Ontario, Canada

Edited by Bonnie Widicker
Designed by Tim Larson
Typeset in 10/12 Century Schoolbook

Copyright © 1992 by
Pacific Press Publishing Association
Printed in United States of America
All Rights Reserved

Library of Congress Cataloging-in-Publication Data:

Padgett, Tricia
   The tempting of Audra Gray / Tricia Padgett.
      p.   cm.
   ISBN 0-8163-1069-6
   I. Title.
PS3566.A32T4   1992
813'.54—dc20   91-31720
                                                                  CIP

92 93 94 95 96 · 5 4 3 2 1

Contents

Chapter 1: 7
Chapter 2: 13
Chapter 3: 20
Chapter 4: 27
Chapter 5: 33
Chapter 6: 41
Chapter 7: 47
Chapter 8: 55
Chapter 9: 60
Chapter 10: 68
Chapter 11: 75
Chapter 12: 83
Chapter 13: 88
Chapter 14: 91
Chapter 15: 97
Chapter 16: 102
Chapter 17: 110
Chapter 18: 115
Chapter 19: 120
Chapter 20: 130
Chapter 21: 136
Chapter 22: 140
Chapter 23: 148
Chapter 24: 153

Dedication

To all Christians with "closed" spouses

A tug of war of the heart.

The Tempting of Audra Grey
by Tricia Padgett

Audra Grey was an easy target for emotional disaster. Her marriage of many years was lonely and sterile.

One day a sensitive man offers her all the attention and intimacy she so desperately craves. In the midst of fierce temptation, Audra discovers that God will open doors to emotional and spiritual freedom if we just trust Him.

US$8.95/Cdn$10.75. Paper.

To order, call toll free 1-800-765-6955, or visit your local ABC.

© 1992 Pacific Press Publishing Association 2492b (2467)

Chapter 1

Eagerly Audra Grey swept into her office and glanced at the Monday-morning manuscripts stacked atop her desk. The "slush pile" sat off-kilter like a literary Leaning Tower of Pisa.

"Or Tower of Babble." Audra chuckled to herself, smug at inventing a simile and pun so early in the day.

Settling onto a high-backed swivel chair, she picked up the first manuscript. The drab manila envelopes were as inviting to her as colorfully wrapped gifts at Christmas. Every editor's dream lay buried among those manuscripts, the dream of discovering gold, the story, the bestseller of the year—or decade, perhaps.

But the first packet proved an instant disappointment. "Handwritten!" Audra uttered the word with annoyance and frowned at page 1, which abounded in grammatical errors. Nevertheless, she would treat this fledgling writer gently. After all, not too long before, the editor herself had felt the stout blow that only a rejection slip can deliver straight to the spirit.

She reached for a note pad and scrawled a directive to Marie, her secretary. Having designed several unique letters, Audra had stored them in the secretary's computer. There they waited to print kind messages that would let writers down easily, not snuff the hope that often barely flickered alongside gangling creativity.

After sticking a memo on the package, she added, "Please include my class handout on typing a manuscript."

"Perhaps that'll help," Audra said under her breath, brushing aside the tailings of guilt that came every time she practiced this ritual of rejection.

THE TEMPTING OF AUDRA GREY

Manuscript two raged with kamikaze pilots and gunfire. The editor's practiced eye skimmed over the pages, searching for some inspirational threads. Sighing, she reached again for the note pad. Marie would print a message reminding the writer that this was a Christian publishing company, dealing with biblical principles applied to everyday living. While the story was, indeed, well written, it would fare much better with a secular publisher, the letter would advise.

"Strike one, strike two," Audra murmured, picking up the next story. "And will you strike out?" she asked the plump package. "Hmm! A heavy one!" she noticed.

Her heart fluttered a little when she detected the few telltale ragged edges of computer paper. "Maybe we've got a pro here," she hoped. But the cover letter dampened such prospects when it began:

Dear Miz Audra:

The enclosed manuscript, *Eddie Mae and Me*, is true.

The editor glanced at the postmark. Blowing Rock, N.C. She was familiar with the town of rambling rock walls and evergreens just off the Blue Ridge Parkway. Audra had grown up forty miles south of there in Hickory, North Carolina.

The cover letter also mentioned the author's master of arts degree in English "among other learnin'." Then he concluded,

If ya need to get ahold of me, I'm sorry but I don't own a phone. I do jeep to town twice a week, though, to teach a class and to visit the local post office.
I'm looking forward to your reply.

It was signed in bold black ink—Craig McGregor.

"An artist's hand," Audra speculated, "and a real mountain man." She dreaded turning the page to more of what she termed "hillbilly jargon." To her surprise, however, a musical flow of prose followed, prose that kept her interest locked from the first sentence. Mr. McGregor was a wrestler of words. He tamed them

CHAPTER 1

and used them with the skill of a true craftsman. And Mr. McGregor was a psychologist as well, Audra noted, pulling her along, toying with her curiosity, then coaxing her to turn the page.

> When Eddie Mae was seven and I was nearing twelve, mountain laurel suddenly burst into blushing bloom amid the deep emerald of "thickety bresh," as my kinfolk called it.
> Her long blond locks stuck out like scarecrow straw. Her green eyes spit fire that nearly drowned in the tears she held back, not daring to blink. And I, with the wisdom of a sixth-grade Solomon, slew her foes with one verbal blow: "My grandpappy says fellas tease girls only cuz they're sweet on 'em!"

Moments later Audra tore herself from the next page and pressed a button. "Marie, I think we may have a winner here. While you run off a couple of photocopies—and it's a long one—I'll finish the slush pile."

"Be right in!"

The secretary spirited off Mr. McGregor's story while Audra attacked the dozen or so manuscripts remaining. She found only one more of promise, then lugged the pile into the other room, plopping them down on the desk.

A polite "Thanks!" came from Marie as she handed her boss another stack of papers, the fresh copies neatly crisscrossed.

"I'm not to be disturbed," Audra ordered, joking, "unless there's a tornado warning or something."

Marie nodded.

The editor pulled out a footstool and settled down again, this time with her stockinged feet propped up. Leaning back, she continued reading *Eddie Mae and Me*.

It was the love story of two country youngsters who married in a country church, then left the country for the city and an education.

> Our time belonged to others now, not ourselves. The few moments we stole were spent longing, longing for the mountains tucked beyond the horizon, for the serenity of

THE TEMPTING OF AUDRA GREY

snowflakes, for solitude, for woodsmoke winding heavenward with our prayers.

Rare were the occasions when they could slip away to a canoe that rippled through swamp waters, "where we felt free to giggle and act foolish, far from stern-faced professors who would surely remind us we were no longer children."

One afternoon Craig abruptly asked his bride, "What're we chasin' after, Eddie Mae? Would you be contented with a house in suburbia, with carpooling and luggin' kids to Little League games?"

In a dreamy voice she had replied, "I'd rather lug any kids we might have up to some mountains and hike where God intended them to play. I'd teach 'em the names of insects and flowers and..."

The couple packed up the next morning and traveled back to their roots, to a wooded crest along the Blue Ridge. There they remodeled Great-grandpappy McGregor's cabin, expanding it into a modern but rustic home, made more cozy with Craig's wood sculptures and hand-crafted furniture. They settled once more into their simple country church, where wedding and baby presents consisted of homemade jams and embroidered pillowcases.

> While I always peered up at the sky, the trees, the mountains beyond, Eddie Mae cast her eyes to the tiny world at our feet, teaching me about "critters" and plants I never knew existed. There on that quiet, peace-filled ridge, we learned from each other and from God Himself, who burnished the skies each morning and evening with His own artist's brush.

Audra stretched and rose to her feet, strolling to the window, where autumn barely showed alongside the concrete and asphalt of Nashville. With manuscript in hand, she paced back and forth across the carpet.

> Thinking she had finally become pregnant, Eddie Mae sought out a doctor, who gave her the truth all too bluntly. Cancer. Only six months to live, maybe longer if she subjected herself to knives and chemicals and other tortures.

CHAPTER 1

> Eddie Mae became seven again, and I was nearly twelve, but this time I couldn't chase off the bullies. I could only wrap my arms around her and sing to her—and love her.

Audra felt the prickle of tears as she guessed the fate of this young woman who had become her friend in the last hour. She reached for a tissue and read on.

Although the ensuing story turned a tragic corner, Craig injected humorous anecdotes that counteracted what otherwise would have been too pathetic a story to read. And through it all he helped his wife feel good about herself, no matter how the medical treatment marred her beauty.

Audra's emotions felt wrung out by the time she read a note Craig had penned to his dying wife:

> If you lose all your hair, that lovely mass of gold, I would adore you in your bald beauty. I'd kiss your head's smoothness each night.
>
> They can chop off both your arms and legs, and I would still marvel at your form.
>
> If the peach softness of your face turned to pock pits, I, who love texture, would adore it and, feeling the roughness with my lips, would tremble joyfully like moonshimmers on a windstirred lake.

"Oh, to be loved that way!" Audra breathed, turning her attention again to the tale.

> The doctor came twice a day now with shots "to make her comfortable." As was our custom, Eddie Mae and I gave each other footrubs in the evenings. But the time came when she could no longer muster the strength to rub even my littlest toe.
>
> "Don't worry, my love! I'll just rub your dainty feet twice as long to make up for it. And I'll powder your baby-soft back with the petals of fragrant roses so your dreams will be filled with perfume."

11

THE TEMPTING OF AUDRA GREY

She smiled the same trusting smile of the seven-year-old amid the blushing laurel.

Audra sat down heavily in her chair, dreading what the final pages would tell her, but unable to stop reading. She had become a part of the story, feeling the couple's pain as if it were her own.

The night stretched to an eternity while we waited for daylight and the doctor.

"Craig," Eddie Mae pleaded with a small voice. "I wanna see the birth of this new day."

I gathered bed quilts about her little-girl body and carried her to the porch swing and propped her head against my chest so she could spy the sun's first rays splash over the eastern mountains.

"Craig," she said more faintly, "you've loved me more than any woman could ever ask to be loved. I've been so blessed having you as my husband." Her voice dropped to a whisper. "Ya know, many folks live to be gray-haired and wrinkled and never experience our kind of love."

I couldn't answer just then. I kissed a bare spot among the smattering patches of blond that still clung as tenaciously to life as my Eddie Mae had. Then a sparrow awoke and greeted us from a branch overhead.

With a smile curling her lips, Eddie Mae took her last breath.

Audra blinked herself back to the moment, to her office, and tried to shake off the sobs that engulfed her. She felt furious with her tears, so uncharacteristic of the dignified editor she was supposed to be. She chided herself for acting like a silly housewife crying over a maudlin novel. "But this isn't fiction," Audra said aloud while pulling another tissue from its box.

Deep down the truth niggled her: *It's not the story that affected you so.* It was envy, she realized, envy for the married love the McGregors had enjoyed. The kind of love the Bible's Solomon and the Shulamite girl had shared. The kind of love Audra and her husband, Hugh, would probably never know.

Chapter 2

Audra reached for her purse and the compact inside. Two large, brown bloodshot eyes stared back from the mirror. Anyone could see she had been crying.

"Oh, well!" Audra sighed and ran a brush through her shoulder-length hair, tilting her head to make certain every black strand had returned to its proper place. "I can't hide here any longer," she decided, "if I want Howard and Jeanette to know about this gem before lunchtime." Then she carefully lifted the copies of Mr. McGregor's manuscript as if they were, in fact, some rare treasure.

Marie glanced up as Audra emerged from her office. "I'll be down the hall awhile. Any calls?"

The secretary handed her a few notes. "I'll take care of these after dinner," she promised, then smiled a thank-you.

Audra found Howard deeply engrossed at a computer screen. His thin, scholarly face wore wire-rimmed spectacles that were forever creeping down his long nose. But the eyes held compassion, and Audra realized she had sought Howard's support first because of that compassion and his lighthearted disposition. "Jeanette won't be as cooperative," she predicted.

Setting the manuscript on Howard's desk, Audra rocked slightly on her heels like a little girl about to ask her father for a favor. "May I intrude?"

"Sure!" He looked up and grinned, obviously noting her red eyes. "You must have a real tear-jerker there, huh?"

"It'll win prizes for sure." Hesitantly, she ventured, "Howard, I need you in my corner when the committee meets Thursday.

THE TEMPTING OF AUDRA GREY

Could you take time to read this manuscript before then?" She handed him one of the stacks.

"How can I turn you down, Audra?" Howard said graciously. "You always take time to go over my great discoveries."

"Thanks!" she replied, adding, "You might find Mr. McGregor's theology a bit liberal, and in places it even borders on pantheism. Also, he occasionally wanders off on tangents that don't really move the story forward."

Howard's graying eyebrows shot up at the statement, but Audra rushed on. "I think with a good job of editing, though, this book could become a classic."

He shook his head while chuckling. "A classic? When will you ever stop viewing the world through those rose-colored glasses of yours, my dear?"

"Probably never," she answered lightly. "That optimism fuels my spirit, you know." Turning to leave, Audra thanked him again.

On the other side of the room divider, she nearly bumped into Jeanette.

"Uh, I've been eavesdropping," the tan-haired woman confessed, "and I'm interested. What's the 'take-away'?"

Audra eased into a chair and thought a few seconds before replying. "The take-away is to appreciate and care for your loved ones while they're here instead of waiting until the relatives all crowd around the casket later."

Jeanette looked unimpressed. "That theme has been overworked recently." In silence, she read the first few pages while Audra watched her face for a reaction. Everything about Jeanette was socially correct: her poise, her neatly manicured fingernails, her tailored clothes—all the graces that made Audra feel like an imposter. She was a newcomer, an English and religious-education teacher, who had somehow wandered into the publishing industry by chance.

"Hmmm! Mr. McGregor does have a unique style," Jeanette admitted. "There's real poetry here. Is *Eddie Mae and Me* true?"

"He claims it is." Audra waited while the other woman examined several more pages.

CHAPTER 2

"OK. I'll read it before the big powwow on Thursday, but don't get your hopes up. The fall lineup for next year is pretty full. I doubt this would have a chance."

Audra straightened her shoulders, gathering boldness. "I was thinking about a March release."

"There's no way this could be ready by next spring."

"The spring after next?"

Jeanette nodded. "Perhaps. But would the author be willing to wait that long?"

"After you've read this manuscript," Audra informed her, "you'll realize that Mr. McGregor is a modern Job!"

"We'll see." As Jeanette returned to the manuscript, Audra realized she had been dismissed.

Back at Marie's desk the editor reported that she was leaving for lunch. After punching a time clock in the hall, Audra entered the women's restroom nearby. Encircled by a blur of gray and soft rose, she washed her hands and splashed cool water on her face. Scrutinizing the image in the mirror, she noticed her eyes were looking more normal now.

Moments later Audra clicked briskly through the lobby, pushed open a glass door, then jaunted down the steps and out to her car. Pulling off her high heels, she slipped her feet into athletic shoes for her usual noon walk.

A smattering of young trees brightened her path as their copper-colored leaves drooped, then stirred in a light breeze. Her hair, too, was tossed about by the wind. But Audra didn't feel its chill. Parts of Craig McGregor's story churned through her head, reminding the woman of the giant void in her own marriage.

After a half-hour walk, Audra returned to her small car and the small lunch she had packed in an equally small ice chest. She relaxed and ate leisurely in the sun-warmed vehicle. The publishing house was perched on a hillside overlooking an avenue busy with noontime commuters. Beyond the street stood a few rundown houses amid some scraggly trees. And beyond them, higher hills loomed in various stages of autumn array, encircling Nashville.

If the city weren't so far from her family, Audra thought she would like living there. Nashville's climate stayed mild most of

15

THE TEMPTING OF AUDRA GREY

the year, and on the east side, where she worked and lived, the traffic was tolerable. Rarely did she venture downtown. But when she did, Audra enjoyed the sights and sounds native to the Southern city, which, she believed, possessed a charm all its own.

"If I could just share it with Hugh or the kids," she thought. But those days were gone. Nearly out of college, her children would be on their own soon. Already they returned home on only a few weekends and holidays.

"Will I ever get used to my empty nest?" Audra wondered as she tucked a yogurt carton into a litter bag. Some of her friends back in Knoxville liked to tease her about becoming a grandma "someday," but Audra thought that time waited too far off. Right now her arms seemed to crave a small body to cuddle and love. *Maybe it's not just a little person I long to hold.*

Quickly she switched off the thoughts and reached for her high heels. Now she became Audra Grey again, acquisitions editor, prepared for the rest of the day.

After work she guided her car along the thoroughfare back to the freeway and gazed wistfully at the restaurants passing by. Audra hated Monday evenings. If she could just stop and treat herself to a good meal, that would help speed the long, bleak hours that lay ahead. Then she could easily glide through the rest of the week. Tuesday evenings she led a women's Bible study in her neighborhood; Wednesday evenings she attended prayer meeting at a local church; Thursdays she packed her suitcase and anticipated going home; and every Friday she made the three-hour journey east, back to Knoxville. There her house waited on a wooded hillside in the outskirts of the city. But on Monday evenings Audra was forced to face her solitude, and it clung to her like an ugly shadow.

When another restaurant flew past, she slowed, weighing the possibilities. She and Hugh had put themselves on the tightest of budgets in order to keep their two children in a Christian college. Then their son, Andy, would enter medical school the following year. Because Hugh considered a restaurant meal a frivolous expenditure, Audra decided to drive on home and face her silent kitchen—again.

CHAPTER 2

She recalled a few years earlier, when income from Hugh's accounting business had failed to stretch enough to cover hefty college bills. It was then, through a church friend, that Audra had found the editing job. At the time it seemed heaven-sent. But as the months, then years, rolled on, her life seemed increasingly bleak, far from the people she loved. She reminded herself that the situation wasn't permanent, but would last only until the kids finished school.

Ironically, Audra delighted in the job that separated her from her Knoxville home. She liked editing almost as much as she had enjoyed teaching in junior college years before. And she found most of her Nashville friends amiable enough.

"But I feel like I'm playacting on weekdays," she told herself, "as if I'm caught in a strange time warp." Then her real life resumed again during the fleeting hours between Friday night and Sunday afternoon in Knoxville.

Old oaks and rosy brick greeted Audra when she turned her car into her apartment complex. A sudden wash of sadness chilled Audra as she collected the newspaper and mail, then gazed up at the second story. It wasn't the meager thrift-store furnishings that depressed her—the lopsided sofa or rickety bed. She never cared much for fancy things. It was the stark loneliness that seemed to haunt the place.

"Well, here it goes!" she breathed, stepping inside and ascending the stairs to face another dreaded Monday night.

Abundant work made Audra's week more bearable. And by Thursday afternoon she felt heartened when she took her place at the large committee table.

Although Audra felt anxious about her projects that would soon bear the scrutiny of this group, she usually welcomed such meetings. They offered not only variety, but also camaraderie to an otherwise sedentary and sometimes solitary job.

Such committee meetings could also offer what she called "sanctified contention"—Paul-and-Barnabas-type disputes that flared up occasionally. They reminded her how easily secular power plays could enter their Christian world if they lost sight of evangelistic goals. For the most part, however, the committee

17

members remained strong in faith and mild in temper, a comfortable setting for Audra, who avoided confrontation.

After the heads of various departments reported on the progress of projects in their areas, the discussion turned to new manuscripts. Finally it was Audra's turn to present her proposal. "This is a first-time submission," she began, "*Eddie Mae and Me,* the true story of two country youngsters who go off to the city to pursue an education, then discover they've left a gold mine in their own backyard up in the mountains of western North Carolina."

Audra became increasingly animated as she gave a synopsis of the story, then read a few brief excerpts. At last she said, "It's evident Mr. McGregor is a master of words. I think we've got a prize-winning manuscript here, one that we should consider seriously."

"And I agree," Howard chimed in. "I've read the entire manuscript, and it wasn't hard to do, despite its length."

Audra smiled, then acknowledged Jeanette, who wanted to speak.

"I, too, was impressed with the story. But as Audra pointed out earlier, McGregor's faith is a bit liberal, and sometimes, because of his enthusiasm for nature, he wanders off course." Jeanette studied the pen she twirled with her slender fingers. "I believe the manuscript should be edited with a fine-toothed comb. And such editing will take some time with one this long. And the editor should know the Bible thoroughly—"

Howard cut in. "Most of us do, Jeanette." Then he leaned forward and addressed the group more earnestly. "Audra here grew up just south of Blowing Rock, where a good portion of the story took place. Also, I might add that she minored in theology and is probably the most religiously conservative of us all."

Because of the approval in Howard's tone, Audra mutely accepted his last statement as a compliment. Then she heard him suggest outright that she be appointed editor for *Eddie Mae and Me.*

Across the table, Tim Blackwell shook his balding head and spouted, "Hold it! We haven't even agreed that the manuscript should be accepted."

CHAPTER 2

Others nodded in agreement.

"Also," Tim continued, "what publication date are we considering, anyway?"

Meekly, Audra suggested, "Next fall, perhaps?"

Jeanette didn't hesitate to contest. "That's impossible. Our lineup for next fall is already complete."

Howard played peacemaker. "I have an idea. Why don't we vote to accept *Eddie Mae and Me* pending the author's response to a spring publication date—the spring after next, that is."

"What if Mr. McGregor decides he'd rather try another publisher instead of waiting?" Jeanette asked.

"We'll cross that bridge when we come to it," Howard told her.

Audra smiled inwardly at his response while watching hands being raised around the table in favor of *Eddie Mae and Me*. She settled back with relief, assuring herself that this manuscript would outsell every other title but the Bible. Then she recalled Howard's question the other day. Was Audra simply wearing her rose-colored glasses again? She cringed at the thought. No. *Eddie Mae and Me* would be a winner. No doubt about that.

As soon as the meeting was adjourned, Audra rushed back to her office and dictated a letter. "Dear Mr. McGregor," she began.

Chapter 3

Audra's car nosed through Friday's five-o'clock traffic, then zipped off the freeway at the third exit. A few more turns, and the wheels rolled to a stop in front of the familiar apartments.

Audra dashed up the stairs, grabbed a suitcase and shopping bag, checked the thermostat, then raced back to the car and returned to the freeway. This time she would continue east on Interstate 40, leaving Nashville behind.

The first mileage sign told the traveler that 163 miles lay between her and her destination of Knoxville. Reflected in Audra's rearview mirror was the image of a Confederate flag decorating the grill of a semi. Seconds later the truck roared past, buffeting her little compact.

But now, except for the humming of the engine, she rode in silence as the sun sank behind her. Audra wanted to capture the spectacle of a country autumn before twilight tucked it away for the night. But time was against her.

Enough scrub pine and red cedar speckled the hillsides to offer dark contrast to the bright gold of hickory and rich bronze of beech. Scarlet oaks and maples blazed against the muted yellows of papaw and elder. Audra sighed, wishing she could travel earlier, when the sun's rays dipped deep into ravines, revealing the spicy colors of ironwood and birch swelling out of a cornucopia of maroons and golds.

A restaurant sign jetted out of the trees, telling travel-weary families about their playground just ahead. Audra smiled, thinking how welcome such a sign would have been to her and

CHAPTER 3

Hugh years before after their children had been cooped up in the car for hours.

Momentarily her heart stirred with pride at the thought of her children. Natalie, so much like her mother with her dark hair and large eyes. Andy, blond like his father, but sensitive and outgoing like Audra. They were staying true to their childhood faith, although even in a Christian college that faith was challenged occasionally. And in spite of their part-time jobs to help with tuition, both young people managed to maintain high grades. Natalie was undecided about her career choice, but Andy kept his heart set on becoming a doctor.

The sun was tinting the hills ahead of Audra, casting its final glow on the higher country she was heading into. Then she spied the next sign:

Carthage 24
Knoxville 150

Off to Audra's right, evergreens clustered together. They looked spindly and small, too crowded for proper growth.

"Maybe if Hugh and I lived together all the time, if we became really close, we wouldn't grow either. Maybe we'd just turn into spindly Christians, blocking out any light from God." Then Audra laughed at herself. "Waxing philosophical again!"

The headlights illuminated another sign:

Cookeville 30
Knoxville 129

She knew this sleepy high country was a multicolored mural now, with autumn at high pitch, but she could barely discern the outline of the hills.

Billboards displaying pictures of Western wear poked bright rectangles in the dark. "Must be a lot of cowboys in Tennessee," Audra guessed, "or people who like to play cowboy."

And what are you playing, Audra? Mrs. Hugh Grey. Perfect wife, perfect hostess, perfect Sunday school teacher and church member, while your life grows more joyless by the day.

Cookeville 15
Knoxville 114

Now the billboards were tempting her with visions of food as she neared the midpoint of her journey. When hunger pangs began to

21

THE TEMPTING OF AUDRA GREY

gnaw at her stomach, Audra reached for the sandwich she had packed. She didn't want to slow the pace until she reached the rest area where she usually got out and walked a few minutes.

When lights from remote houses twinkled from the hillsides, Audra found herself drawn to the humanity around her, although they couldn't actually respond.

A sardonic smile twisted at her lips. But wasn't that what her life had become? A reaching out without the response she craved—ever since her best friend, Julie, had moved away. Michigan might as well have been another planet. Because Hugh despised long-distance phone bills, Audra had tried writing. But Julie had recently gone through a painful divorce and wasn't replying often.

Audra sent her friend a card occasionally to let her know she still kept Julie in her prayers. Then Julie surprised her with a cassette tape of praise songs—the cassette that was playing in the car stereo at that very moment. And as Audra sang with the tape, she thought of her best friend, so far away, so alone now without her husband.

"Maybe I should be more thankful for what I do have," Audra lectured herself, "and stop dwelling on the negatives. After all, I'm usually a positive person." Hadn't Howard noticed her "rose-colored glasses"? If Julie were still in Knoxville, though, she would guess the truth, that Audra's bubbling façade hid a hurting woman.

Another sign: Cookeville 1 mile.

"Hello, Cookeville! Goodbye, Cookeville!" Audra called as her car sped past the exit. "Someday I'll stop and visit you," she promised. Hadn't someone told her that the time zone changed just down the road? She needed to set her watch an hour ahead. A whole hour was suddenly ripped out of her life. But she would gain it back on Sunday evening.

A new thought popped into her mind. Craig McGregor would have stopped in that town. He would have taken the time to browse through its shops and chat with its people.

"Not at this time of the night!" she argued. "I doubt if anything's open."

The road sign told her that only ninety-seven miles remained to Knoxville. "Down to double digits," she breathed, feeling fatigue tug at her shoulders.

CHAPTER 3

The air chilled now as the road climbed higher. Now she was the one passing trucks as they crawled up the steep incline. The miles blurred past until a sign announced that Knoxville lay only sixty-five miles ahead. "I'm almost to the rest area," Audra reminded herself.

When she pulled into the parking area and eased out of the car, she groaned at the stiffness in her joints. The security lights shone brightly through white oaks. Their leaves would turn rust colored in a few weeks and cling stubbornly to the branches. "Very few of them will drop off," she noted, remembering the year before, when the rusty leaves clung to the trees throughout winter. *The trees are like me—partly dead, partly alive. But will my spring ever come?*

The visitor's center was welcoming, with brochures filling racks about the room. Audra selected a few, thinking, "Perhaps Hugh and I can visit these places someday."

She looked wistfully at the flyers in her hands, advertising scenic places in the Great Smoky Mountains, historic Jonesborough, Gatlinburg. Remembering that Hugh also classified vacations as frivolous expenditures, Audra admitted, "We never will." Carefully she replaced the brochures in the proper slots.

Back on the road, Audra came upon a construction zone and slowed to the suggested speed. "Legalist, that I am," she remarked.

But Audra looked inside her own heart. Was she walking the "narrow," strictly keeping civil and moral laws with as stony a heart as the Pharisees in Jesus' time? She considered the question a few moments. Then her mind traveled back to a vivid scene in her childhood.

She and her friend, Jenny, had been placed on a pew in the empty sanctuary while Audra's mother visited with the minister in his office. The eight-year-olds sat quietly, staring up at a picture of Jesus' crucifixion. Audra even remembered the mixed fragrances of the empty church, the smells of new carpet, withering flowers, and furniture wax. And she remembered her empathy with the tortured figure on the cross. Deep grief had cut into her tender heart, and she sobbed, "He did it for us, just so we could go to heaven someday."

THE TEMPTING OF AUDRA GREY

When she had finished describing Jesus' suffering to Jenny, the little friend added her tears, bringing Audra's mother on the run.

Audra smiled at the remembrance. No, she wasn't a Pharisee. As far back as she could remember, she had truly loved Jesus.

Lord, is it Satan who has separated me from Hugh and my children? Or is it the result of my own response to circumstances? Or did You allow this to happen for a reason? Maybe I'm some kind of female Job, undergoing a strange test? She determined to study Job again, maybe during the long evenings in Nashville.

Harriman 12
Knoxville 49

In her weariness the miles slipped by unnoticed. There was the fork, Chattanooga to the right, Knoxville to the left. She was closing in on the last miles home, and she could feel elation rising within her, masking the weariness.

Finally she was passing the motels and restaurants that seemed to fringe every city and town along the interstate. The number of billboards increased, all vying for her attention. But her attention was focused on home, the sprawling tan-brick house nestled in the side of a hill on the eastern outskirts of the city.

Because traffic was light that time of night, Audra decided to stay on I-40 instead of taking the bypass around Knoxville. High wires towering overhead looked to her like giant robots holding up umbilical cords of the city. Then came a quadruple overpass, gray cement and steel intertwining. Street lamps glowed over Victorian- and Colonial-style homes, reminding Audra of the cardboard houses she played with as a child.

Back then she had been so full of little-girl dreams about her future, about the Prince Charming who would ride off into the sunset with her. The sardonic smile returned to her lips. Hugh was hardly a Prince Charming, but at one time she had been totally smitten by him, his blond hair, his eyes that, chameleonlike, seemed to change color, even to lavender at times, depending on the color of his shirt. He was handsome and sure of himself, witty, but shy in crowds. She knew that shyness had attracted her. It had made her feel nurturing and protective.

Ah! There was her exit. Then right onto Millertown Pike. Past the East Towne Mall, where she and her children had come

CHAPTER 3

often, the closest thing to "city" her children knew. She chuckled. Because of her sheltering ways, Andy and Natalie were basically country kids, and she was pleased with the outcome. Her headlights picked out the driveway as it wound up a slope to a garage. The dog bounded to the car, barking in greeting. Then she opened the front door.

"Hugh!" she called.

She heard a muffled voice from the kitchen. Dropping her suitcase in the entryway, she went in search of her husband and found him at the sink.

"Hi!" she sang as she hugged his tall, trim form. "Did you have a good week?"

He grunted a reply and gave her a dutiful peck on the cheek.

"Oh? Trouble again with the thrifty threesome?"

Hugh's forehead creased into a scowl. "Doctors are so pompous. I think they play God so much, they begin to think they're Him."

"Hugh!"

"Well, it's true. They're getting more and more impossible to work with. And frugal. They're so tight they squeak."

Audra kept her tone cheerful. "Doesn't that make your job as an accountant easier?"

"Not really."

"Well, the other doctors you deal with are pretty agreeable, aren't they?"

"I suppose." Hugh's words sounded flat, so unlike the eagerness she felt.

Audra followed Hugh into the living room. He picked up a church magazine and took refuge behind it, answering her questions in one or two syllables. Audra tried a bit longer to draw him out, then gave up. She felt too weary.

She dragged herself to the entry and lugged her things off to the bedroom. On the desk lay her mail, and she took a few moments to shuffle through it. "The book I ordered!" She unwrapped the book on communication in marriage.

A few minutes later she was engrossed in the first chapter, stopping now and then to call to her husband, "Are you coming to bed, honey?"

"Uh-huh," he would mumble, his hollow voice filtering down the hallway.

At last the print began to blur, and Audra put the book on the bedside table. With a defeated sigh, she turned out the light and nestled into her pillow, staring into the blackness. The sad realization stared straight back: *I'm just as lonely here as I was 160 miles away.*

Chapter 4

When Audra awoke, the sun had already crept over her windowsill and was peeping through a slit between the drapes. She yawned, reminding herself it was an hour earlier back in Nashville.

"Car lag!" She giggled, throwing on a robe. She found her husband finishing his breakfast in the kitchen.

"There's some toast left over if you want some," he said.

"Thanks!" Audra yawned again. "I had hoped to wake up earlier so I could fix you a real Southern breakfast for a change."

"Why?" he asked bluntly.

"Well, I like to play housewife once in a while." Audra poked a playful finger at his ribs and declared, "You're becoming so independent, Hugh Grey, a regular crotchety old bachelor. I do believe you've gotten used to waiting on yourself."

"Maybe I have." Then she lost him to the front page of the *Knoxville News-Sentinel*.

Oh, well! I caught his attention a few moments—and he did offer me some toast. That shows he cares, at least a little. The bright fall sunshine beckoned to her. "This would be a good day to spend outside."

"Uh-huh."

She had so much work to catch up on that the day passed at the same brisk pace at which Audra raked the leaves in her front yard. She wore loose-fitting navy slacks with a sky-blue sweat shirt, a Christmas gift from Natalie.

Because "World's Greatest Mom" was blazoned across the front, Audra felt reluctant to wear the shirt in public, where

THE TEMPTING OF AUDRA GREY

people might consider her a braggart. On the other hand, she had no qualms about modeling it before the nonjudgmental eyes of her friends, the birds and squirrels.

Standing in a patch of sunlight between two stately chestnuts, Audra rested briefly against the rake handle. As she had watched Hugh methodically digging some bulbs from the flower bed, she composed a story for him.

In snatches that morning, she had read more from her new book on communicating.* The author suggested creating "word pictures" that would illustrate to her mate how she felt.

Because Hugh enjoyed gardening, Audra decided to use a garden theme. The plot consisted of a small tree that needed lots of water, weeding, and care in order to grow. But the gardener ignored the tree until it finally withered and died.

That evening she quickly typed up the tale and brought it along on their trip to a church business meeting. In the dim light of the car, she read her creation to Hugh.

When Audra finished, she asked, "Well, what did you think of the story?"

"I thought it was terribly sad. The poor little tree withered and died."

"Then you understood its meaning?" she asked excitedly.

"Of course! If you don't water small, struggling trees, they'll die." Her husband looked pleased with himself as he pulled the car into the church parking lot.

"Oh, Hugh!" Audra's ire rose, and she could hear the mocking tone in her own voice. "Can't you see what I'm trying to tell you about us?"

"Us?" He gave her a perplexed look. "Frankly, no."

"OK, let me explain. I'm the little tree."

"Audra," her husband countered, his voice now edged with irritation, "you are not a tree."

She sighed in exasperation. "Pretend I'm a tree!" she begged. "You are the gardener." When she noticed his eyes darting nervously around the parking lot at the other cars pulling in, she spoke in rapid sentences. "Hugh, I feel parched, not for water, but

---

* Gary Smalley and John Trent, *The Language of Love* (Pomana, Calif.: Focus on the Family Publishing, 1988).

CHAPTER 4

for your love. There I'm stuck in Nashville, far from you all week. I miss you so much I can hardly stand it. When I come home, you practically ignore me. I'm lucky to get a kiss from you. You rarely phone during the week to let me know you even care I'm alive."

"Phone calls are expensive," he defended himself.

She ignored him and continued, "I'm so starved for affection, Hugh, that I feel like that tree must have felt just before it died."

He turned and faced her, not really meeting her eyes, but gazing somewhere over her right ear. "You feel that bad, huh?"

Her "yes" sounded more like a whimper.

"Hmmm! What do you want me to do?" he asked in his usual monotone.

There was a moment of frozen silence before she replied, "Well, for starters, I'd like to get hugged more. It would be nice if you actually looked happy to see me when I arrive home on Friday nights. And I need a phone call from you after prayer meetings on Wednesdays."

"Every week?" he asked, surprised.

"Of course!" She smoldered silently a few moments, then regained her composure. "Hugh, don't you ever get lonely in that big house without the children and me in it? Don't you ever get to missing me when I'm gone?"

He scratched his chin. "To be honest, I don't think about it much. I keep pretty busy at work and stay there until awfully late at times. I'm usually so tired I go right to sleep when I get home at night."

She could tell he was growing nervous about getting inside in time for the meeting. Then his arm shot around her and gave her a quick squeeze. "There! Now let's go in!"

That evening Hugh draped his arm around Audra, and she settled into its crook, feeling perfect bliss. *Maybe the word picture is working.*

Later, on their way home, Audra told her husband of a report she had read about some babies who died because they weren't held. "People need a certain amount of physical human contact each day," she said. "If that's true, honey, then because we're apart so much, we've got a lot of hugging to make up for on weekends."

THE TEMPTING OF AUDRA GREY

In response, Hugh pulled her close, and they rode cuddled all the way home. Embers of hope flickered anew within Audra.

But the next morning those embers were abruptly snuffed out when she awoke to the old phlegmatic Hugh. "He acts as uncaring as the computers he works with," she thought sadly. "Maybe if I had a keyboard attached to me, he'd pay more attention."

Dressed for church, Audra waited in the living room, reviewing a few Bible texts. Suddenly, Hugh stood before her. With the sandy hair and finely sculpted face of his Teutonic ancestors, he looked incredibly handsome. And her heart fluttered girlishly when she peered into his eyes. They matched the color of the denim blue suit he wore.

"Ready to go?" he asked.

She admitted to herself that her husband was, indeed, the most handsome man in her church—perhaps all of Knoxville, she decided, but quickly wilted. What good were those looks when the man behind them refused to share himself with her? He was like an exquisite statue that could be enjoyed only from afar.

The car retraced its route of the night before. About fifteen minutes later Audra spotted the church, its tall Doric columns blazing white against red brick in the morning sunshine. An archway separated the church from the elementary school—the same school her children had attended when they were young. The place held many memories. She had loved the drives to and from school. They were times of sharing with Andy and Natalie about small daily incidents that made up their childhood. Those times had drawn them close.

Smiles came easily as Audra and her husband stepped inside the church. As if on cue, the charade began: Hugh with outstretched hand to welcomers, shyly charming, uttering all the appropriate phrases. No one detected the steely core under his soft Southern manners. And Audra, just as guilty, went along with the act the couple had polished so craftily over the years. She thought she played the role of "contented wife" quite well, the way she leaned demurely on Hugh's arm and tried to project the image of glowing happiness.

Unexpectedly, she felt small chubby arms embrace her knees fiercely. She looked down at three-year-old Christy, whose

CHAPTER 4

shiny, pale hair was fastened with a pair of pink ribbons. The upturned face grinned crookedly at her. "Hi, Missus Grey!"

"Good morning, sweetheart! Are you on your way to your Sunday school class?" Audra asked.

"Yes, ma'am."

Audra bent down to give the little girl a send-off squeeze and felt her heart warm with the gesture. What would she ever do without her loving church family, without such spontaneous bursts of affection? "I'd probably shrivel up like the poor tree in my story," she concluded.

Audra took a deep breath and determined not to allow Hugh's coldness to drain her of her innate joy for life. If she weren't careful, she could turn into an empty husk that no longer appreciated such delightful things as Christy-hugs.

After teaching an adult Sunday school class, Audra sat stiffly beside Hugh in "their" pew, facing the backs of the rest of the congregation.

There was pretty, slim Mary with her deaf daughter, coaxing the girl to the place between her parents. Then her other child, Mike, the victim of an automobile accident, hobbled on crutches to his place nearby.

Audra then gazed over at Gail with her retarded son, nearly grown now. Another couple guided their daughter's wheelchair down the aisle.

Why so many, Lord? Couldn't Satan pull these beautiful Christians from Your straight path by his usual means, so he was allowed to smite their children? Is it some kind of character-building process we all must pass through in order to leave the dross behind?

"Let's all stand and sing the Doxology," came the voice from the pulpit.

Audra rose to her feet with the others, Hugh looking woodenly ahead like a soldier in a military parade.

"Praise God from whom all blessings flow!"

"How can Mary and Gail sing so spiritedly?" Audra wondered. Their joy made her feel almost guilty for having two strong children, both healthy and scholastically gifted.

She glanced over at the elderly Maggie Thorpe. The poor woman was riddled with cancer and probably wouldn't last

31

THE TEMPTING OF AUDRA GREY

much longer. "Monday she goes back to the hospital," Audra remembered. "I must talk with her after church today." The week before, Maggie had expressed some doubt about her own salvation, and Audra needed to go over the simple verses that led a person to Christ. She knew that once the elderly woman reviewed those verses, her doubts would flee. "Sometimes people complicate the gospel," Audra thought, "when it's actually quite simple—and free."

When the song finished, her eyes strayed back to the crippled youngsters in the congregation. *Is this man at my side—this man who promised over two decades ago to love, honor, and cherish me—is he the equivalent of the others' handicapped children? Has some demon wrapped long talons around Hugh, keeping him "closed" to me? Is another demon named Workaholism taking off during these holy hours, only to return later to rob us of quality time together—time for sharing, for leisure, for intimacy?*

Perhaps Hugh was just as crippled—only without a wheelchair. His spirit didn't even have crutches to hobble around on, she thought.

Suddenly an overwhelming pity welled up within Audra. *Poor, poor Hugh! You're missing so much of life.* How she longed to help him! But none of her efforts had worked thus far. Still, Audra, the "rose-colored glasses lady," continued to hope.

"As many as can, please kneel for prayer," came the voice again.

Maggie Thorpe had stopped kneeling months ago, Audra noted as she glanced again at the white-haired woman, whose sallow skin, once plump and ruddy, now sagged from her stooped frame. "I must talk with her," she repeated.

Pastor Jim's prayer began, but Audra couldn't concentrate on his words. How many times over the years had she prayed—begged God? And still, no change. *My poor, crippled husband. He's missing his own life, Lord.*

Chapter 5

Tuesday evening Audra followed her flashlight beam up the hill toward the next apartment complex, where her weekly Bible study met. A dappling of moonlight reflected off the oaks, stark and black, spreading their bony arms into the night.

Except for an occasional passing car and the soft crunching of her shoes on the leaves that seemed to carpet everything now, a deep quiet lay over the neighborhood. Lights winked from the myriad of windows above, apartments built to resemble a medieval castle, its towers and turrets forming a Gothic outline against the hill. Then higher still, another building rose, it too reminding her of knights and nobles and kings.

When Audra resumed her hike up the steep slope, an amusing idea flitted through her head. "They're all looking down upon my serf's quarters in the hollow." She cast an affectionate glance back over her shoulder. The apartments did resemble servants' quarters compared to the luxurious estates above. "But the neighborhood is nice, and rent down there is low," she mused, "well within Hugh's strict budget." Of course, the rental rates rose as the apartments climbed higher up the hill. But Audra didn't mind living in her plain brick "servants' quarters" as long as they remained clean and comfortable.

She recalled how pretentious and out-of-place the medieval architecture had seemed at first, set down on the fringe of a Southern city. But then she considered the strong Anglo-Saxon roots that ran deep in the populace, especially up in the hill country.

THE TEMPTING OF AUDRA GREY

"So why shouldn't they reach back into their past and pull out a castle or two?" she asked herself. Then, quite suddenly, she was peering into the round, freckled face of Kathie Miller.

"So there you are, Audra!" the young hostess drawled as she took the other woman's jacket. "We were beginning to worry about you. You're usually the first one here."

"I'm sorry. Guess I was just daydreaming and dawdling."

Kathie laughed. "Well, this is a good neighborhood for that."

The friendly voices of four more women, a Bible resting on each lap, greeted her in the living room. There was Sylvia, an amused expression on her black face, which, Audra knew, could instantly fill with extraordinary compassion. The eldest of the group, Anna, sat in the corner. She neared sixty, but looked younger in a girlish way, her gray eyes intense and lively.

Shy Jenny, a single mom, sat beside her small son on the couch. Jenny's blue jeans were covered with an assortment of stuffed animals, books, and tiny toy vehicles to keep the boy amused. Audra's gaze lingered on Jenny. She had made amazing spiritual progress in just six months, and Audra hoped she would be baptized soon.

"My mother came through surgery wonderfully," the remaining member, Trudy, announced. Hair the color of honey swished about her face as she explained, "The doctors were amazed at her fast recovery and sent her home much earlier than expected. She's doing great." Trudy giggled. "And that's why I'm here tonight instead of at her house."

"Praise the Lord!" resounded around the room.

"And what about your husband's job?" Audra asked Sylvia, whose smile quickly faded.

"It's still up in the air," she said. "I'd like us to pray about it again tonight."

Then Kathie questioned Audra, "And how is your friend with cancer?"

"I got the chance to go over some scriptures with her on Sunday," Audra told the group. "Maggie had mentioned some doubts as to whether she was truly a Christian or not, and here she's been a member of our church for years! Anyway, when we finished reviewing the verses, I prayed with her." Audra's voice

CHAPTER 5

trembled at the remembrance. "The sweet lady cried and clung to me with such gratefulness. There are no doubts left about her salvation."

Amid delighted voices, Kathie asked further, "And the cancer?"

"She was supposed to go back to the hospital yesterday," Audra said. "I won't find out until I get home next weekend if Maggie was able to undergo more chemotherapy. Her blood count was pretty low—" Audra looked uncertainly from one face to the other. "You know, Maggie's already suffered so much. I think we should simply pray for God's perfect will to be done in her life."

The others responded with polite murmurs and nods, then knelt with her around the coffee table.

Audra longed to open her heart to these women, to tell them about her loneliness and about Hugh. But she decided against such disclosure. After all, most of them were "milk Christians," and Audra was supposed to be mature in the faith, an example to them.

After prayer Audra opened her Bible and began their study with, "Let's all turn to where we left off in the Gospel of Mark. I'm not an artist," she said, "but if I could paint a picture of Christ's life on earth, I'd place His agony in Gethsemane smack in the center, with other events encircling the scene."

"Even the crucifixion and resurrection?" Anna asked in surprise.

Audra smiled at her. "Well, it's true our futures would look pretty bleak if Christ hadn't risen from the dead. But a battle raged in Gethsemane that night, a battle between good and evil, between Jesus and Satan. And the fate of the entire human race hinged on the outcome." Audra looked into each face, her tone sober. "Because this portion of Scripture contains some really heavy truths, I'd like to spend at least two sessions on this part, maybe longer." She took a deep breath and said, "Kathie, would you please read Mark 14, verses 32 through 34?"

Kathie's plump fingers found the page. Then she read: " 'They went to a place called Gethsemane, and Jesus said to his disciples, "Sit here while I pray." He took Peter, James and John along with him, and he began to be deeply distressed and troubled. "My soul is overwhelmed with sorrow to the point of death," he said to them. "Stay here and keep watch" ' " (NIV).

35

THE TEMPTING OF AUDRA GREY

Audra let everyone digest the words before she repeated, "'Stay here and keep watch.' In another Gospel, John uses the word *abide* forty-one times, then twenty-six times in his epistle. 'To abide' in this context means 'to stay.' That's what we do here every Tuesday night—although many of you have jobs all day as I do, and you must feel awfully tired by seven o'clock."

"Oh, but I wouldn't miss this time for anything," Trudy cut in. "This time with y'all seems to refresh me and help me get through the rest of the week."

Audra smiled at Trudy's enthusiasm. "I feel the same way." Then she addressed the group again. "Before we get into the really heavy subjects, let me ask you something: Have you ever stopped to think that Jesus, who was the very Deity Himself, longed for human companionship? Here He's practically begging His disciples to stay with Him, to help Him through this terrible time."

Anna interrupted, "But a little later Jesus said that was for the disciples' sake, so they wouldn't 'fall into temptation.'"

"True," Audra agreed. "But as I search the Scriptures, I find a real longing on the part of Jesus for fellowship, especially here at Gethsemane, where He got a foretaste of bearing the sins of every human being who ever lived and will live."

Audra then asked the youngest member, "Jenny, what three disciples did Christ choose to accompany Him into the garden?"

"Peter, James, and John," the girl responded and added, "the same dudes who climbed Mount Trans-something with him."

"Right! The Mount of Transfiguration," Audra said, pleased that Jenny had remembered. "Those three disciples were special to Jesus, and that's why He needed them close to Him at such a trying time."

"Well, they weren't so great," Jenny blurted, "because they kept falling asleep." The girl suddenly looked embarrassed by her outburst.

Audra was quick to remark, "I'm so glad you brought that up, because there's a great lesson for us here. Remember, Satan and his legions of demons were in that garden too, and I'm sure they had something to do with the disciples' heavy eyelids." Audra paused and put on her most serious face. "But I honestly believe

CHAPTER 5

that if Peter, James, and John had just hung in there and had forced themselves to continue praying, that God would have refreshed them. Then those three men could have had the marvelous privilege of comforting their Master. After all, think of the many times He had comforted and prayed for them! Now they had the chance to do the same for Jesus. Instead, they fell asleep, and God had to send an angel."

"What angel?" Jenny asked.

"Luke tells us in chapter 22 that an angel appeared and strengthened Jesus." Audra clicked her tongue. "How sad! Peter, James, and John missed a real blessing—all because they didn't pray just a little bit longer so their prayers could have fought back the powers of darkness."

Kathie spoke up, "And that's how it can be for us, huh? We might not give in to temptation so easily if we would simply hang in there and pray longer."

"Yes!" Audra cheered, then directed them to the next verses. She delighted in such study. For her it was like digging for buried treasure and finding small gold coins that increased in size and value as the digging progressed.

That evening's session continued until Audra looked at her watch a final time and closed the meeting with a brief prayer.

Picking her way through the dark later, she thought about Gethsemane, about Jesus' need for empathy and comfort, about her own need to open up to someone. Again she wished for her old friend, Julie. "I could talk frankly to her, without worrying about disillusioning her or hurting her Christian experience," she thought. "But Julie lives in Michigan now."

On Thursday of that week, Audra was surprised to receive a letter from Craig McGregor, agreeing to the publication date. As soon as the editor finished reading his note, she dialed Howard's extension.

"Mr. McGregor has given us the go-ahead."

Howard's congenial voice shot back, "Great. I think you've definitely found a bestselling author in that mountain man."

Audra felt elated. "Then I may go ahead and send him the usual contract?"

THE TEMPTING OF AUDRA GREY

"Right."

She replaced the receiver with a smile of triumph, then dictated a short letter to Mr. McGregor that would accompany the contract. She added a postscript about a few of her theological concerns about the manuscript.

The next day Audra spent glued to her computer as she edited part of an inspirational book for women. When the clock reached five, she was ready to drive straight home to Knoxville. She wouldn't even take the time to stop by her apartment on the way.

Three hours later, she could hear the phone ringing as she unlocked the front door. Breathless, she answered it.

"Audra, did you hear the bad news yet?"

She recognized the voice of Pastor Jim, and at once her mind began to race frantically. *The house is empty; Hugh isn't here. Has something happened to him?*

"Maggie Thorpe died today."

The words fell upon Audra like hammer blows, and she heard a small wailing sound. Was that her own voice?

"She just fell asleep. No pain."

The rest of the conversation blurred as she tried to steady herself. Pastor Jim asked if Audra would be willing to sing two numbers for the funeral on Monday, and she replied that she would have a tough time, but would try.

"I'll call someone this weekend," she offered, "and get permission to go back to work on Tuesday instead of Monday." She remembered how much Maggie had loved to hear her sing. "I even made a tape for her once, Pastor, to listen to in the hospital, some of the old hymns."

"Really?" The minister obviously detected her sorrow. "I'll talk to you Sunday about which songs you choose to sing." Then he mercifully said goodbye.

Audra crumpled into a chair. The pent-up loneliness, the longing, the frustration, all the sadness of the past few weeks seemed to explode within her, and she burst into sobs. "Oh, Maggie! Poor, poor Maggie! How I'll miss her!"

In that moment she wished her parents would walk through the front door. Her big, broad-shouldered dad wouldn't hesitate. He would rush to her and throw his strong arms around her. And

CHAPTER 5

her short, round mother would join in. Her mom had always known what to say when a parakeet or a kitten had died. And if the couple ran out of words, they would simply cry with her.

That thought brought a faint smile to Audra's lips. At the sound of Hugh's car coming up the gravel drive, she dashed into the kitchen, tossed cold water on her face, and patted it dry with a dish towel. Then the front door opened, and Hugh stepped inside, carrying his briefcase.

"Hi!" she said glumly, shuffling to his side.

"Hi!"

"Maggie Thorpe died today."

"I heard," he said, glancing toward the living room. He didn't even look directly at her. And if he had noticed her red-rimmed eyes, he didn't mention it.

She clutched him, saying, "I feel devastated. Maggie's been a dear friend for years."

"Audra," Hugh said with some impatience, pulling himself free of her and heading for the easy chair where some papers lay. "Maggie was old, and old people die."

His wife stood limply in the center of the room, like a deserted child, silent for a good two minutes. She could feel new tears rising from some deep pit inside her.

"Hugh," she ventured, "Maggie's death has shaken me to the core. I need comfort. Won't you comfort me?"

His puzzled expression topped the page he was reading. "What do you want me to do?"

"Just hug me."

He sighed, put down the news, pulled himself up, then enfolded his arms stiffly around her.

Audra felt as if she were being hugged by a store manikin.

"There! Is that good enough?" Hugh asked, obviously eager to get back to his reading.

"It's enough," she said, tears still threatening.

She made her way down the hall to the master bedroom and her desk, took out a piece of stationery, and began to write.

Dear Mr. McGregor,
    Today I lost a friend—Maggie.

THE TEMPTING OF AUDRA GREY

Audra wrote about the little lady's courage and endurance, about her own anguish, every drop of it, then reread the letter. When she finished, she quietly tore it up and dropped it into the wastebasket. Audra would never share such intimate thoughts with a stranger—and especially not with a male stranger. But somehow she knew that Craig McGregor would understand.

As she changed clothes, she remembered her words to the Tuesday-evening study group: "Have you ever stopped to think that even Jesus longed for human companionship? . . . He practically begged His disciples to stay with Him, to help Him through this terrible time."

After crawling wearily into bed, Audra turned out the light. It was Friday night, her room was dark, Hugh was still reading at the other end of the house—"missing another blessing," Audra thought, "just like Peter, James, and John."

Chapter 6

Monday after the funeral Audra dropped by a library and checked out some books from the psychology section. Then she pointed the car westward, eager to enjoy any leftover autumn beauty along the drive back to Nashville.

Making the drive earlier than usual gave Audra the chance to view the sunset from a different vantage point. Rather than frowning into a glaring fireball, she chose to park her car and linger awhile, watching the colors change along the cloud-streaked skyway. In that peaceful setting, the tension that had mounted during the funeral gradually ebbed away.

"But I'll never forget Maggie Thorpe," she whispered, taking comfort in the memory of their last conversation together, of Maggie's glad tears. "She had such spunk, such courage," Audra recalled. "She was a fighter." Then the sudden realization came to her, "And I'm a fighter." She smiled, wondering if that shared tenacity was the glue that had bonded their friendship. *But Maggie never knew about my real struggle.*

Safely back at her apartment, Audra began to study the books she had selected. First she read about the "closed man" in *Why Can't Men Open Up?** "In this headlong pursuit of the 'idealized self,' a man's 'real self' is often lost—and so is the possibility of intimacy."

"How depressing!" she thought, then examined a section about the workaholic, discovering that he can hide so well from

---
*Steven Naifeh and Gregory White Smith, *Why Can't Men Open Up?* (New York: Clarkson N. Potter, Inc., 1984), pp. 154-164.

THE TEMPTING OF AUDRA GREY

his own feelings that nothing short of a crisis will force him to face those feelings.

"But that's a pretty drastic way to get a person to change," Audra murmured, then recalled that some of the greatest Bible characters had to face crises before they made changes in their lives. Samson, David, even Paul struck down on the road to Damascus. She read on, studying the traits of a workaholic. Noting a certain few—his constant preoccupation with work, his inability to enjoy leisure—Audra contended, "This only partially describes Hugh."

On some occasions her husband took time out for the family, especially when the children were home. "And Hugh's a great father!" she acknowledged. He had always given both Andy and Natalie the attentive listening they needed and had discussed every detail of their concerns with them. Audra admitted, however, that Hugh seemed comfortable limiting the talk to facts, not feelings. The children usually shared feelings only with her, their mother. Otherwise, Hugh could easily win the Father-of-the-Year award. And Audra supposed his devotion to Andy and Natalie had helped the youngsters become so well adjusted.

Then the thought jolted her: *It's me! I'm the one he ignores and acts preoccupied around. Could I possibly be intimidating him somehow?*

More questions riddled her as she finished skimming the pages, then went on to read from another book, *The Fantasy Bond.**

Dr. Firestone, the author, described how couples can start off feeling real friendship and caring for each other, but then develop a fantasy bond, which he called an "effective painkiller to relieve their fear of aloneness and lessen the ache of hunger." He claimed that those in a bond "avoid closeness and *real* affection and instead form strong dependency ties." His next words made Audra shudder: "Unable to accept the reality of their lack of feeling, they attempt to maintain a fantasy of enduring love." That was exactly what she and Hugh were doing—maintaining the fantasy of Mr. and Mrs. Grey, happily married couple!

---
*Robert W. Firestone, *The Fantasy Bond* (New York: Human Sciences Press, Inc., 1985), pp. 49, 58, 133.

CHAPTER 6

She turned the page and read, "The absence of personal feelings, eye contact, etc., give an observer the strange impression that this person is not totally present in his own body." Thinking about how Hugh rarely looked her in the eye, Audra shut the book with a thud. "This person is not totally present in his own body." The words reverberated through her mind.

"That's Hugh, all right. But I'll not willingly keep up the act," she defended herself. "I crave a genuine relationship with him." Audra knew she would settle for Hugh's touch, his listening, his caring—ordinary, not spectacular, things.

Then the words of Eddie Mae returned: "Many women live to be gray-haired and wrinkled and never experience our kind of love."

Suspecting that very few couples shared the kind of intimacy Craig and Eddie Mae McGregor had shared, Audra evaluated her own situation. She was blessed with much—a nice-looking husband, two healthy and accomplished children, friends, an attractive home, enough food, cars, and "things," even a wonderful job and a fulfilling ministry in her church and neighborhood. Shouldn't that be enough to satisfy any woman? Was she guilty of coveting something she wasn't meant to have—the true affection of the person she married?

Audra glowered at the unopened volumes before her, then scoffed at herself for playing lay psychologist. Gathering up the books, she stacked them all neatly by the front door and vowed to take them directly to the library in Knoxville on her way home the next Friday. *No more self-diagnoses!*

The days spilled into one another. Then on Thursday shortly before noon, Audra informed her secretary that she would be spending the afternoon in downtown Nashville at the library. "I've got some research to finish before this manuscript is ready to release for typesetting," Audra said.

Moments later Marie's voice twittered over the intercom, "Is there a Miz Audra on the premises?"

"Oh, is Mr. McGregor on the phone?" the editor asked.

"No. Actually, he's right here."

Audra felt strangely lightheaded. She was about to meet the promising new author. "Please send him right in!" she ordered.

43

THE TEMPTING OF AUDRA GREY

In strolled a powerfully built man about her age. He wore a blue sports coat, well-tailored navy slacks, and cowboy boots. His thick dark-auburn hair was not quite as well trimmed as the mustache and beard that half-covered his face.

Surprised by her pounding heart, she managed to say in a modulated voice, "Mr. McGregor! I'm so very pleased to meet you." She stood to shake his hand, the hand of a Goliath, then looked into the palest blue eyes she had ever encountered. They seemed to hold her in place momentarily, and she winced inside, faintly embarrassed.

"It's my pleasure, I'm sure," he returned, apparently unaware of her discomfort.

Audra motioned to the chair near her desk. "Please, sit down!" Then she asked, "Did you receive the contract yet?"

"That's why I'm here," he said, reaching inside his jacket for an envelope.

"Oh?" Audra's heart seemed to drop to the pit of her stomach. *Trouble with the contract*! She tried to act nonchalant. "Is there some problem with it?"

"No problem at all, ma'am!" His accent was quite apparent now, truly "mountain" the way his tongue lingered lazily on each syllable, as if he had all the time in the world. "Because I was going to be in Nashville anyway, I thought I'd drop the contract off in person."

Audra breathed a silent sigh of relief as she took the two papers from him and looked them over. "As soon as the director signs these, I'll return your copy—along with a check, your advance against royalties."

"There's no hurry," he said, smiling as if he knew some deep secret about her.

Audra suddenly felt awkward and groped for a thread of conversation. "I don't mean to pry, but you said you have other business here in Nashville?"

"As a matter of fact, I do," he drawled. "A while back a Nashville fellow came visiting up at Blowing Rock. He spied some of my wood sculptures on sale in town and decided he'd like to carry my work in his store here."

"How nice!" Audra remarked.

CHAPTER 6

Mr. McGregor chuckled. "Well, to be honest, I'm not sure if it's nice or not. That's why I'm here with my portfolio instead of a truckload of my carvings. I'd like to look at his shop first, then talk business—perhaps."

She was curious. "Why so cautious?"

"Well, I'm not used to dealing with flatlanders, ma'am, and I've heard tales."

The editor stifled a smile at the word *flatlanders*. Mr. McGregor was definitely not an imposter. Despite his education, he remained a true mountain man. "You didn't seem to hesitate about signing this," she said, pointing to the contract on her desk.

"No, ma'am. You're a person I can trust."

Audra felt her eyebrows rise. "You could tell that by the few words I wrote?"

He shrugged and unabashedly proclaimed, "Of course! I'm a good judge of character."

"I imagine you are, Mr. McGregor. And I hope our working together on your manuscript won't change your impression of me."

"I doubt that it will. You'll find I'm pretty easygoing." Then the man referred to his watch, saying, "My relatives near here are expecting me for dinner before I venture downtown. So I'd better be going."

They both rose to their feet while Audra mentioned, "I'm venturing downtown myself, to the Ben West Library this afternoon."

Craig McGregor looked triumphant. "Why, the library isn't too far from that fellow's shop. He said it was down a few blocks from there. Would you mind giving me directions?"

Audra took out a clean sheet of paper and drew a map. "Actually, the best way to see downtown is to park your car—Jeep, wasn't it?—at Rivergate Park, then ride the trolley wherever you want to go. It's fun."

"They have trolleys in Nashville?"

"Well, they're actually little buses made to look like antique trolleys. But if you ignore the sound of the motor, you can actually imagine yourself back almost a century," she told him.

"The trolley it is, then!" he decided and thanked her for the map, again taking her hand in his massive one. "I appreciate your time, Miz Audra, and look forward to working with you."

THE TEMPTING OF AUDRA GREY

"Likewise," she said for want of any other response.

He paused in the doorway. "Ma'am, you had mentioned some things about my manuscript, about pantheism and stuff."

"Yes?"

"I'd like to have the chance to talk with you about that. Do you have any time tomorrow morning—early?"

Audra flipped the desk calendar and frowned. "Actually, I don't. There's a staff meeting. I'm sorry." Then she remembered, "We'll both be downtown this afternoon. Why don't you stop by the library, say, about four? I should be finished with my research by then. I'll take along a copy of your manuscript."

"How do I find you?" he asked.

"I'll be in the reference section."

"Sounds good! I'll see you then," he said and was gone.

Audra marched back around her desk and tried to gather her wits. Although she had remained calm in Craig's presence, her heart had raced the entire time. She felt angry at the frenzied feeling chasing around inside her. She had noticed a twinge of pain when he left, but then welcomed the excuse to see him again later. And was that guilt she felt? Why did she feel guilty? She was just meeting one of her authors to discuss his manuscript—in downtown Nashville with its trolleys and riverboats and architecture that whispered of ancient Greece.

Chapter 7

Audra skipped her usual walk, ate a quick lunch in the car, then joined the midday traffic. Once off the freeway, she watched buildings grow taller with each block, a hodgepodge of Colonial and Victorian and sleek, modern styles.

Just as she reached Riverfront Park, Audra spotted a bright red trolley crossing the street toward her. "If I hurry, I can catch that one," she breathed, hastily parking the car.

Overhead a dozen flags flapped noisily as she raced through the wind. Climbing aboard the trolley, she dropped coins in the appropriate slot and slid onto a varnished pine seat. She glanced about at the bus in cute disguise—at gleaming brass poles, the leather straps, and wooden seats. Such ornate decor did, indeed, send her back a century and seemed to coax her to relax a few moments. Soon the driver announced, "Here's your stop."

Toting her briefcase, Audra crossed the street to the glass doors of the library, then walked directly to the reference section and requested some files.

Engrossed in her work, Audra didn't notice the hours slipping by or the large man who sat down across the table from her. But she soon became uncomfortably aware of someone watching her. She glanced up, and the instant Craig McGregor's pale eyes met hers, Audra steeled herself against the rush of confused feelings she knew would come.

In her most businesslike whisper she informed him, "I'll be with you shortly, as soon as I return these."

THE TEMPTING OF AUDRA GREY

An amused expression accompanied Craig's soft, slow syllables, "Don't hurry on my account. I've got all evening."

Audra could feel him watching her intently as she hurried across the room to return the files. She thanked the librarian, then returned to the table and Mr. McGregor.

In subdued tones the editor wasted no time in opening the discussion about sections of his manuscript. "I can well understand your love of nature," she began, "because my father used to drive us up to the Blue Ridge Parkway in the fall, and then again in spring when the laurel bloomed."

"And the flame azaleas and—"

"Yes, it was all so breathtaking," she cut in crisply.

McGregor frowned. "Were you raised somewhere near Blowing Rock?"

"Way down in Hickory."

"Oh?" He chuckled. "Hickory's considered the 'big city' to us mountain folks."

She returned his smile, relaxing a little. "And a person from Nashville would probably consider Hickory a small town." She deliberately thumbed through the manuscript. "I admire your love of nature, but at times that love spills over and saturates your faith a little too much." To his puzzled expression, she explained, "You see, sometimes there's just a hairline between worshiping the Creator and worshiping the created."

"And you think I come across as worshiping the created? To be honest," he said, "I find the two are sometimes intertwined."

She unconsciously tapped a pencil against the table. "I guess we differ on that point, Mr. McGregor."

"Please call me Craig."

"All right. Craig, I believe God made this beautiful world for us to enjoy—and He truly is the Master Artist—but I think we have to be careful to what we give credit and praise."

The man seemed to weigh her statement before requesting, "Can you show me an example from my manuscript?"

"Sure!" she said, turning to a section where the author had described his awe for a sunrise. "In this paragraph, you almost seem to be worshiping the sun itself. My husband once did a study on the sun worshipers of ancient—"

CHAPTER 7

"Your husband?" Craig interrupted, then pointed out, "but you're not wearing a wedding ring."

"No, I'm not," she said softly. "You'll also notice I don't wear any other jewelry either, except my watch."

"And it's quite plain."

"Quite."

He leaned closer, scrutinizing her face. "And you don't wear much makeup either?"

"Not much."

"Does all this have something to do with your faith?" he wanted to know.

Audra nodded. "Yes. I believe the Bible instructs women to wear the adornment of beautiful characters instead of jewelry and makeup."

"Well, you really don't need them," he murmured.

Audra thanked him. "You're kind." Then she explained further, "You see, I feel it's important that nothing comes between God and me—especially not something I wear." Then she realized how sanctimonious she must sound and decided to add, "Not that I condemn others for wearing jewelry or whatever. It's just a personal thing."

Craig nodded slowly. "Yes, I can understand that." Then he grinned. "And I thought some of the Christians up my way were strict—no liquor, no dancing, no bright clothes, no smiling—but you seem even more conservative than they."

"Oh, I like bright colors," she defended herself. "God made a myriad of colors for us to enjoy. And I do smile and laugh a lot." Suddenly she caught herself swept up in the conversation and brought it to a halt with, "Shall we get back to your manuscript?"

They bent over the pages the rest of the hour, then packed up their briefcases. "There's so much more to discuss," she told him, "and that'll come up over the weeks as I edit your manuscript." Then Audra apologized. "I don't want you to think I'm nitpicking, Craig. I do admire your unique writing style. It's just that I want every word to be perfect. Actually, I'm very excited about this story. I think it'll be a real inspiration to many, reminding them of what's truly important." She glanced nervously out the window. Audra knew she needed to exercise, to do something

49

THE TEMPTING OF AUDRA GREY

with the energy churning inside her. "Now if you'll excuse me, I had wanted to walk around the capitol grounds awhile before it gets too dark."

The mountain man looked aghast. "Someone as pretty and fragile as you traipsing around all alone?"

"Oh, I'm sure it's safe," she said. "Anyway, I've got some pretty devoted guardian angels."

"Do they have a black belt in karate?" he countered.

"What?"

"I asked if they knew karate."

She giggled as he followed her toward the exit. "I'm not sure."

"Well, if you don't mind, I'll help your angels out. Here, I'll even carry your briefcase," he offered. And before she could object, he reached over and took it from her hand.

Once on the sidewalk, Audra inquired, "When did you learn karate, anyway?"

"Oh, I did a stupid thing after Eddie Mae died. I joined the army."

"Why do you think that was stupid?"

"Well, I sort of put my grief on hold for three years; then I had to deal with it when I returned to Blowing Rock. I think it would have been much easier on me if I had grieved at the proper time." They crossed the street to Legislative Plaza and began their stroll around the complex.

"Grieved at the proper time." Audra wondered if it was grief she was feeling of late, grief about Hugh and their dying relationship. And was she guilty of putting that grief "on hold," as Craig McGregor had? "I understand about the need to mourn," she told him, "but you should never belittle the fact that you served your country. We Southerners put a lot of stock in that, you know."

"Yes," he chortled, "and I think we North Carolinians are even more patriotic than these Tennessee folks."

"Sssh! Don't say that too loudly around here," she warned, adding, "Do you realize that both states even have red, white, and blue license plates?"

"Yep!" He laughed. "That's patriotic, all right!" Then he admitted, "The army did help me to see the world. I've roamed all over Europe and parts of the Far East."

CHAPTER 7

"How fortunate!"

They continued their walk in companionable silence. Audra had picked up speed, trying to keep up with Craig's longer legs. The couple strolled under an archway in the War Memorial building and entered a long colonnade. Audra hurried over to the statue of a bronze warrior and read the inscription on its pedestal:

> In memory of the
> sons of Tennessee
> who gave their lives
> in the great war
> 1914-1918

She felt a briefcase brush against her as she and Craig stood soberly gazing up at the Greek warrior. In spite of muffled traffic sounds and a few late workers rushing past, for a brief time Audra felt sheltered, as if she lingered in some tranquil oasis far removed from the city's hubbub.

Craig's voice broke the spell. "We have a similar memorial at the city park in Blowing Rock—a large plaque with the names of all our fellows who died in the various wars."

"Yes, our states are quite patriotic," Audra repeated. Then she turned and strolled on across the courtyard and down some steps toward two reflecting pools surrounded by bare trees.

She sighed. "We should see this in spring."

"I'd like that," Craig replied, bringing a flush of embarrassment to Audra's face.

"I didn't mean to imply—to suggest—" she stammered. "I just thought with everything in bloom—"

She stood looking helplessly at him for an eternal moment and was struck by the extraordinary gentleness and understanding in his face.

"I know," he said.

To cover her discomfort, Audra prattled on about the state capitol building they could now see perched upon a dusky knoll across the avenue. "That building was built before the Civil War," she told him, "and the architect was so caught up in this work that he asked to be buried in the capitol wall."

"How do you know that?" Craig asked.

She laughed. "From a report one of my kids did long ago."

Craig naturally asked about her children, and she welcomed the opportunity to tell about them.

They were heading back to a trolley stop when Craig inquired, "And what does your husband do for a living?"

"He has his own accounting business. Most of his clients are doctors."

"Hmmm! Tell me, Miz Audra, are you hungry?"

"Well, I don't usually have much for supper, maybe a salad."

"Then let's find a restaurant, and let me treat you."

She cringed. That would be like a date. This whole thing was getting out of hand. "Truthfully, Mr. McGregor, I don't feel comfortable eating a meal at a restaurant with a man other than my husband."

He laughed. "You are a prude, aren't you?"

She smiled, nodding sheepishly.

"You're hungry?"

She nodded again.

"All right. Then let's walk to a restaurant. You sit down at one table, and I'll sit at another. Then we'll happen to notice each other and begin to talk like old friends. Maybe you could pretend I'm a woman. Would that help?"

"It might." But to Audra's amusement, she knew his hefty build and curly beard would stump her imagination.

They found a small cafe and before long were wrapped in deep conversation over a couple of chef salads. Craig had mentioned again his disdain for flatlanders. "Last summer my friend, who owns a store in Blowing Rock, had to put up a sign to let customers know that only thirty dollars was kept in his safe overnight. Can you imagine that?" He clicked his tongue. "Why, if just us mountain folks were allowed to live in peace as we have for years, my friend would never have had to put up a sign like that."

"Are you saying that hillbillies are honest, but city people aren't?" Audra asked.

Craig looked instantly insulted by the word *hillbilly*. "Ma'am, there's just as big a difference between hillbillies and mountain

CHAPTER 7

people as there is between mountain people and flatlanders."

"Oh?" She stretched out the word with a teasing lilt.

"Yes. Mountain folks tend to be very honest and self-sufficient. In fact, they'd rather starve than go on welfare. But a hillbilly probably wouldn't think twice before he'd take a handout from anybody."

"I see."

Then Craig shared his longing for "Grandpappy McGregor days," back before "rich flatlanders began to clutter the cliffs of Blowing Rock with their fancy summer homes."

Audra smiled. "Do you realize that technically, I suppose, I'm a flatlander?"

McGregor's eyes caught the glint of the restaurant's soft lights. "No, Miz Audra. You may have been raised in the flatlands, but you've got a mountain woman's heart."

"Why, thank you, sir! I consider that the epitome of compliments." Then she announced, "I really must go and catch a trolley back to my car."

Later, sitting across from each other in the quaint seats of the trolley, she said, "I must confess, Craig, that I've learned a lot about mountain folk today. I'm afraid I had stereotyped them as boisterous, illiterate people with little to offer." She glanced beyond him at the stores and banks they were passing. "But I've learned that the contrary is true—if you're any example."

"It's funny you should say that," he chuckled, "because when I was in the service my sergeant tried to get me to yell, but I couldn't. I didn't know how."

"Really?"

"Yep! And my superiors said I could easily work my way up the military ladder if I could just learn to raise my voice. But, you see, a mountain man loves quietude. Oh, he'll laugh and even giggle. But if you make him angry, he'll just go sudden on you."

"Go sudden?"

"That's when he'll get real quiet, then, without warning, will simply shoot ya dead."

Audra's mouth dropped open. "I'll keep that in mind, Mr. McGregor."

He grinned. "The secret is to keep an ear out for that quiet.

THE TEMPTING OF AUDRA GREY

When a mountain man clams up, you simply back off before it's too late."

The trolley pulled up to Riverfront Park, where cars now crowded the parking lot. Audra could see two brightly lighted riverboats moored below them, and colorfully dressed people were milling about on the deck of one. "Oh, look at the riverboats. Can't you just imagine Mark Twain standing there, so at home in his white suit?"

"As a matter of fact, I can," Craig said. "Come on! Let's go down for a closer look!" He took hold of her briefcase again and trotted down the steps to the cement walk below.

The old-fashioned paddlewheel overwhelmed Audra with nostalgic feelings she couldn't quite understand. "This is so— so—"

"Southern?"

"Yes, Southern!" Then her voice dropped. "Craig, I've really enjoyed my time with you, but I must be getting home."

"Don't you want to linger awhile and stroll along the river?" he coaxed. "Or perhaps you'd go to the Parthenon, the art museum. I heard it's open until eight tonight."

A fluttery feeling tugged at her again. "I'd like to, Craig. But I just don't feel at all right about this."

"Audra, the prude?" he teased.

She giggled. "Once a prude, always a prude!"

"Yes, ma'am," he said, shuffling his feet like a scolded child.

Back at the parking lot and their vehicles, Craig handed her the briefcase and squeezed her fingers around the handle. "Good night, Miz Audra! You take good care of yourself."

His kindness and concern for her suddenly loomed in bold contrast to Hugh's indifference, and she had to turn away quickly before Craig noticed the pain contorting her face. "Thank you! Good night!" she called back over her shoulder.

Chapter 8

On the interstate headed east, Audra switched on the radio just as a broadcast minister was preaching, "Don't try to fight the temptation in your own strength! You won't win," he warned. "Instead, ask God for His power to overcome the temptation. Pray immediately."

Audra cringed again. Was God trying to speak to her through this program? Had she sinned in thought tonight? She didn't think so. Was it evil to have joined Mr. McGregor for supper? She didn't think that was sinful either. But she had felt lighthearted and soothed and admired in the mountain man's company. Perhaps there was something prideful about that, she considered.

Therefore, when Audra knelt beside her bed that night, she prayed, "Lord, if I've offended You in any way today, please forgive me." The picture from her childhood of Jesus hanging from the cross flashed through her mind. "I dread the thought of hurting You," she continued. "Help me to deal with Craig McGregor on a business basis only. Help me to think of him as the artist and writer he is—an interesting person, I'll admit—but help me to keep my thoughts about him strictly platonic—and pure."

Audra faced her weekend in Knoxville with new strength and felt that she had won a little skirmish with Satan himself. Her emotions seemed to sail on an even keel until the following Wednesday, when she spotted the postmark of Blowing Rock on an envelope. And in bold red ink the word *Personal* was blazoned across the front.

THE TEMPTING OF AUDRA GREY

Marie didn't seem to notice, however, and her boss thankfully retreated with the letter, her heart pounding anew.

Dear Miz Audra,

This is a formal thank you for your company Thursday evening in the big city.

I hope I'm not overstepping myself, but I must tell you how breathtakingly elegant and lovely you looked as we chatted in that cozy cafe. And I adored strolling with you earlier through the plaza. A magical evening!

Anyway, ma'am, I honestly think it will do you no harm to know that an artist with wise eyes perceives you as the beautifulest woman he's ever seen (and he's teched foot to four continents). You're country sweetness with sophistication. Naiveté coupled with genius. I wish I were a bird; then I could serenade at your windowsill each morning, so you'd wake up smiling.

And your soul is beautiful too. I sense much strength, much character there. (And was that sorrow I perceived?) And I look forward to working with you and, I hope, of becoming your good friend.

Respectfully,
Craig McGregor

Audra felt heat rising to her face. She felt angry with herself for ever seeing this man outside the workplace, angry at his compliments, but, strangely, flattered by them at the same time. Never had Hugh said such things. She giggled in spite of herself. "Maybe Mr. McGregor could give Hugh lessons."

No. Something intuitive told her the letter was wrong, improper, and she couldn't let this go any further. Her hands attacked the computer keyboard with the vigor of a jackhammer.

Dear Mr. McGregor:

I just received your kind letter. I'm afraid, however, it's a little too kind. Remember what a prude I told you I am? Well, that prudishness feels very uncomfortable with such

CHAPTER 8

talk. And, I think, perhaps, it would be better if another of our editors works with you on your manuscript.

Sincerely,
Audra Grey

She backed up and typed *Mrs.* in front of her name—"as a reminder," she mused. She printed out the letter, folded it, and stuffed it in an addressed envelope before she could change her mind. Then she erased the letter from the computer's memory.

Later that afternoon, however, second thoughts began to plague her. What if Mr. McGregor would "go sudden" and decide not to deal with her publishing house at all? What if they lost this potentially bestselling author?

"Then I'd lose my job," she thought bluntly, half-smiling at the idea. "And would that be so bad? I would be forced back to Knoxville and Hugh all week long." But getting fired from such a prestigious job would look bad on a résumé.

The postman had already collected the mail; it was too late for her to retrieve her words. She tried to remember them. Were they rude? With doubts chasing through her mind, she felt miserable. "Did I act out of emotion? Oh, how could I have been so hasty?" She decided to rely solely upon prayer and vowed to keep the blunder to herself. "Maybe the Lord can undo this mess I've gotten myself into," she hoped.

Her anxiety had settled considerably by the time a reply from Blowing Rock was placed on her desk at the end of the following week. Shakily Audra opened it.

Dear Miz Audra Pureheart:
Please forgive this stupid clunk of a male dummkopf! Here I have the friendship of a dear, sweet person and the privilege of sharing thoughts with a real live editor, and I louse it up with indiscretions.

Audra couldn't help but laugh at Craig's next ramblings:

I should be forced to walk on hot coals, barefooted, all the way down to Blackberry Cove; tossed into tanks of agitated

THE TEMPTING OF AUDRA GREY

giant lobsters; lashed with a dozen hickory switches braided together; then dipped in honey and left staked out for the ants and scorpions under a scorching sun. . . .

Audra breathed a sigh of relief. Her company hadn't lost this new author. Nor had she lost her job. She read on:

Please keep in mind I'm an artist, and artists search for beauty. When they find so much of it in one place, they simply feel overwhelmed. That's all.

I promise to act "properer" in the future, to keep my delight in you (or the declarations thereof) under wraps. And in case you haven't figured it out yet, underneath this redneck façade, I'm actually both a gentleman and a shy mountain boy who doesn't know beans about seduction.

I also promise to write only business letters from here on. (Well, maybe on those days when the sun is so pure and the shadows so blue and your image rides on my subconscious like a wee ship with silken sails and I feel driven to say something nice, I'll keep it tame—I hope!)

Repentantly,
Craig McGregor

Now Audra's emotions were swirling with hurricane force. Good sense told her to write a polite reply to the man, but still to request that his manuscript be assigned to another editor. While evaluating the alternatives, Audra chewed pensively on her lower lip. Then Craig would think she was incapable of forgiving. And didn't he already suspect her of being too legalistic, like those mountain Christians he had described to her, people who rarely even smiled? She shuddered at the thought of conveying such a negative impression.

"But what about me?" she asked her empty office. "Am I going to be able to read such phrases as a 'wee ship with silken sails' without my heart fluttering like a silly adolescent's?"

Oh, how she wished she could talk with someone about her quandary! But whom could she talk to? Certainly not her husband. Not the women in her Bible study. Not even her pastor. She

CHAPTER 8

was the one who usually ministered to him and his wife, helping them stand against the usual slings and arrows that are hurled at ministers and their families. Anyway, Pastor Jim was so young and inexperienced, and Audra didn't want to disillusion him. She knew the minister thought the world of her husband.

She turned again to her computer. "OK, Mr. McGregor!" she thought. "I'll give you the chance to act 'properer,' but if so much as one toe strays from the straight and narrow, I'll have every right to hand you over to Howard or someone else."

Then she prayed for tact before she began a reply to the author.

Chapter 9

On Thanksgiving Day Hugh's sedan rolled the long miles across a winter-gray landscape to Hickory, North Carolina. But the scenery, as dreary as it was, couldn't dampen Audra's holiday spirit.

For weeks something inside her had yearned for the familiarity and comfort of her childhood home, and now she was heading there, eager and expectant. In the front seat she relaxed beside her husband, who was driving. All of Audra's attention was focused now on the lilting chatter and laughter from the back seat, where Andy and Natalie exchanged anecdotes about college dorm life, friends, and classes.

Even at his age, Andy still loved to tease. "And when, may I ask, will you be receiving your MRS degree, little sister?"

Natalie scoffed at the idea, then unexpectedly turned serious on him. "I've dated several guys this year, but none of them measures up to my ideal."

Her brother's voice, too, took on a serious note. "And what do you want in a husband, anyway?"

"That's easy!" Natalie replied. "Someone just like Dad."

Audra stiffened at the response, then listened as Natalie continued, unaware how every innocent word was wounding her mother.

"Except for one thing," the girl added. "You have to admit Dad doesn't show Mom much affection. My husband has to be an open kind of guy who's not afraid to hug and kiss and express his feelings—you know, tell me I'm beautiful and stuff like that."

CHAPTER 9

"Oh, yuck!" Andy gagged comically, then quickly drew his sister back into a more lighthearted conversation.

But their voices washed over Audra like meaningless babble. "Natalie knows," she brooded. "After all these years of pretending, of my trying to make up for Hugh's lack, our daughter has seen straight through the act!"

The woman glanced over at her husband and tried to read his face. But the bland expression there told her nothing.

Turning off the freeway, they traveled briefly through Hickory on Highway 321 northward—"the route to Blowing Rock," Audra mused, wondering how Craig McGregor was spending his Thanksgiving.

Then the car found its way along city streets guarded by columns of old trees. Audra took in the familiar lawns and hedges and squarish brick homes with cement driveways alongside. They passed her former schoolyard and the library where she had spent many a rainy afternoon. Nostalgia always closed in during the final blocks of the journey, when she glimpsed grandfather oaks spreading over the sleepy street where she grew up. Then her parents' house swung into view, the dormers upstairs, the broad porch with rock pillars.

In moments her children were cheerfully submitting to the unrestrained, tearful welcome of their grandparents. Then came the boisterous reception of an assortment of uncles, aunts, and younger cousins. A few elderly neighbors, who were always adopted at holiday times, sat looking on from a comfortable corner.

When the sturdy arms of Audra's father closed around her, she laughed and hugged him fiercely. "Oh, Daddy! I'm so glad to be home."

"Well, where else would you spend Thanksgiving?" he boomed, his face alive with amusement. "It's tradition, you know."

She loved his cheerfulness. It was contagious, already brightening her mood. Then her mother's musical voice accompanied another hearty hug. The two women stood back in a loose embrace, the mother's eyes seeming to peer deep inside Audra.

"You look like you've lost weight, darling. Is something troubling you?"

"No, Mama!" Audra insisted. "You always say that!"

THE TEMPTING OF AUDRA GREY

"Yeah? Well, this time I mean it. We'll talk later. You're staying, aren't you?"

"Till Sunday after church," Audra reported happily.

Her nose twitched at the enticing, spicy aromas spilling from the kitchen. She would join her mother there in a minute, but first her gaze lingered on photographs that cluttered end tables and walls, even the dining-room door.

Plunging into the kitchen's whirlwind of activity, Audra helped the other women put final touches on the meal and settled a few squabbles between toddlers. Then she coaxed the men from their places in front of the television, where a football game blared.

As the day progressed, Audra mingled with the members of her family, bathing in the warmth of their talk, in the easy intimacy among them. They were a jocular, flesh-and-blood people, uninhibited by rigid manners and customs. And Audra loved them for their openness. Her husband fit oddly into the group in his usual charming and impersonal way.

By late afternoon, she noticed that her facial muscles ached from smiling so much. She giggled, realizing, "My face hasn't had this much of a workout in months!"

Such an unaccustomed outflow of emotion left Audra drained, and she gladly trailed after Hugh up the stairs that night to her old bedroom. Memories flooded her anew when she spotted the handmade quilt at the foot of the bed and the pictures from her childhood still on the walls. There was the same low, sloping ceiling, the same dormer window peering out over the same dark street.

Lying beside her husband, she whispered, "Did Natalie hurt your feelings today?"

"When?"

"On our way here, when she told Andy that you didn't show me much affection and that she wanted her husband, in that one respect, to be different from you."

"Hmmm! I must have been thinking about something else, because I never heard anything like that."

"Doesn't it bother you that our own daughter recognizes how little attention you give me?" Audra asked.

"Not really. It's just the way I am, and she's certainly not blind."

CHAPTER 9

Silence filled the room. Audra could hear the final sounds of the day below them, the cat being let out, the clinking of glass at the kitchen sink, soft steps up the stairs.

Then suddenly her father burst into laughter.

"Mom's probably repeating some amusing tidbit little Greggie or Bryan said today," Audra guessed. Then she thought wistfully, "Mom and Dad are such good friends. Even after nearly fifty years they can still find things to discuss." They seemed to share everything. Audra considered their golf and fishing. "They even play together."

How empty her own marriage seemed in that moment. In the dark she could barely detect the outline of her sleeping husband. She pictured Hugh's parents, so unlike her own. She had learned to care deeply for her in-laws, though, in spite of the work ethic they pursued as zealously as their religion. And Audra rarely saw any demonstrations of love in their home.

She recalled one Christmas Day when she had leafed through her in-laws' photo albums. There were pictures of small grimy faces sticking out among cornstalks and tomato vines. There were prints of a miniature Hugh, his pudgy hands clasped around a bucket handle. Then later in life those same hands, much larger, grasped the steering wheel of a tractor.

But where were the photos of fun times, Audra wondered, of building roads with toy trucks, of picnics or outings at a nearby lake? Then the stark reality hit—there were none. She sadly suspected that her husband and his brothers had been robbed of their childhood, of the everyday playtimes children needed to develop their imaginations.

"Poor Hugh!" Audra breathed. "You were never allowed to be a child." The idea brought tears to her eyes. "No wonder you're so driven to work. You've known little else." She gently stroked his still face. *And whoever taught you how to love, my husband?* She knew the pitiful answer.

Then her ponderings took a strange twist. "Maybe Hugh's mom and dad are normal." Perhaps she, Audra Grey, had been spoiled by having such expressive parents who knew the importance of both work and leisure. With more questions plaguing her, Audra finally drifted into sleep.

THE TEMPTING OF AUDRA GREY

In spite of rain on Friday, Audra took a long walk around her old neighborhood. Under a bright blue umbrella she gazed at Oakwood Elementary School. Although it wasn't the same stucco building she had attended much of her childhood, the red-brick walls stood on the same grounds, a short distance from her parents' house.

She felt drawn to the large bell mounted on a sturdy base, a memorial of the original North School, which had been a milestone in Hickory's educational system at the turn of the century. Audra remembered reading that a determined group of women had been responsible for the school's being built.

Overhead, clouds parted and a pale sun peeked out. She looked affectionately at the bell before resuming her walk. Audra had heard stories about a janitor known as Old Lum who would ring that bell continuously until every last student was safely inside the school. It was only because of Old Lum's tender heart that very few children were ever marked tardy.

Three decades later the original school was enlarged and remodeled, and behind its creamy stucco walls, Audra had learned the three Rs. She remembered her sorrow the weekend she had returned to Hickory and found those stucco walls in rubble beside the new red-brick building that still stood today.

Old Lum occupied her mind during the rest of the walk. His largeheartedness was remembered down over the years, even long after his death. "And what will people remember about me?" she wondered. "I could easily evolve into a bitter old woman if I'm not careful." She cringed at such a prospect, an ugly legacy for her children and the generations to come.

On Sunday when her family prepared to leave, Audra couldn't stop the tears from flowing as she hugged her parents goodbye.

"I love you!" her mother said.

Audra felt a rush of gratitude for her mother and her simple statement. "I know," she replied, then climbed into the car.

The Grey family reached Knoxville in time for Andy and Natalie to catch a ride back to college. Then the parents returned to their quiet house. Because of the trip to Hickory, Audra had already asked to have Monday off. Now she sprawled in the

CHAPTER 9

living room, which, despite its cozy clutter, seemed to her like the loneliest, most forsaken place on earth.

Switching on the TV, her husband sat down near her feet at the end of the couch.

"Feeling kind of glum without the children?" she probed.

"Maybe."

"Don't you sometimes wish we could turn back the clock, so they'd be small again?" she asked.

"I don't know."

"Or perhaps we should have had more than two children—a whole batch of them! Then we'd always have little ones running around here."

Mild irritation crept into Hugh's voice. "You've got to be kidding! We can barely support these two properly."

Coincidentally, at that moment the TV commentator was saying, "In 1631, while giving birth to her fourteenth child, the beautiful Mumtaz Mahal, 'Chosen One of the Palace,' died."

Audra immediately became enrapt in the story behind the Taj Mahal, the stunning wonder of the world, which lay on the outskirts of Agra, India. She listened to every word: "The grief-stricken emperor, Shah Jahan, determined to build a mausoleum of the utmost magnificence, 'as beautiful as she was beautiful,' he was reported to have said." Scenes of the glittering white marble structure, then closeups of jeweled inlays followed, while the commentator described in detail the setting and architecture of the Taj Mahal.

When the program ended, Audra sighed wistfully. "It took the emperor twenty-two years to build that memorial to his wife. He certainly must have loved her." Then she took a quick look at Hugh's impassive face and exclaimed a bit too cheerily, "Didn't you think that was terribly romantic of him?"

Her husband shattered the spell with, "I think people have romanticized the whole thing out of proportion. And the emperor mustn't have been too considerate of his wife to have put her through fourteen pregnancies." Then he frowned. "Maybe it was guilt that drove the fellow to build the Taj Mahal. After all, childbirth was what finally killed her."

Audra threw up her hands. "I can't believe you could watch something like that and not find at least one romantic thread in it.

THE TEMPTING OF AUDRA GREY

Do you always have to look at everything with such, such critical eyes?"

"I'm not being critical, just realistic. The world isn't full of romance, Audra. The world's a tough place to live in, and unless we can keep a step ahead of it, we'll end up just like that Mrs. Mahal or whatever-her-name-was. And all the marble-and-gold buildings in the world will never change the fact that she died ahead of her time."

Audra felt a sore lump swelling in her throat. She and Hugh seemed to speak different languages. Wasn't there some common ground between them where they could really communicate, she wondered. As she rose from the couch, there was sorrow in her voice. "It's hard being a right-brained person in a left-brained house." Then she wandered back to her room and took solace in sleep.

When Audra returned to her office Tuesday, the stack of manuscripts and other mail on her desk rose higher than usual. It took her most of the morning to sort through the pile and to reach Craig McGregor's latest letter. After he had reviewed her comments about a certain portion of his manuscript, he wrote, "You never let me know if that was sorrow I perceived in your eyes that evening at the capitol plaza. I'm not being nosy, just concerned."

When she was able to reply to his letter later that week, she added the postscript:

> You're a perceptive person, Craig. When you saw me, I had just said goodbye to a dear friend. In fact, I had sung at her funeral the Monday before. I guess I was still hurting from that. But now I'm OK again. The grief for Maggie's passing has subsided.

The following week there came a reply:

> I'm proud of you. Sprung back like a green birch sapling, unbroken and strong—and ministering once more. Good!
> I'm strong too. But like a rock. Before I allow myself to be bent, I roll away somewhere, where I become solid again.

CHAPTER 9

I can't be as pliant as you. But I admire your strength and tenacity.

Then Craig reminded her of his stint in the service and how he had "put his grief on hold" until he got back to Blowing Rock and the house where he and Eddie Mae "had loved."

My friends recognized the fact that I hadn't grieved yet, and they formed a circle of sorts around me—took turns just sittin' and listenin', noddin' every once in a while. Mountain folks know how important grieving is.

You see, Miz Audra, if you don't let that grief out, then it stays inside and festers, and it can "go sudden" on you later, when you least expect it. Therefore, I'm glad you've grieved sufficiently for your friend, Maggie.

Audra laid the letter aside and felt warmed by the words. Oh, how she wished this mountain man were a woman instead! He would make such a sensitive friend. She wouldn't have to pretend to him. She could be open, and he would understand.

"Yes, I've grieved sufficiently for Maggie," she told herself. But a fear prickled her, the fear that she was holding onto a grief far more destructive, a grief that she had ignored for many more years than Craig McGregor had ignored his. And she wondered, "What kind of a person will I be when this is all over?" But then an even greater dread gripped her. *What if it never is over?*

Chapter 10

The pale December sun brightened the room as Audra sorted tree ornaments. Christmas was hurtling toward her too rapidly.

"I wish I could take time off from work to bake and shop and decorate," she told her husband, who was setting up a good-sized spruce nearby.

"Yeah, and if you did, we could never pay all the bills at the end of the month."

When Hugh finished stringing the lights, he left Audra to trim the rest of the tree. The task took precious time from her hours in Knoxville. "But it's well worth it," she thought, mustering a small smile for her children's delight in Christmas.

Although standing at the brink of adulthood, Andy and Natalie kept a joyful delight in holiday traditions—the cantatas, the caroling, the gifts. "And the crèche," Audra whispered as she gently unwrapped a ceramic figurine of Mary.

Setting up a miniature stable, she placed each figurine carefully around the manger. All the while she considered how like the little clay figures she had become. Audra couldn't quite pinpoint the moment, but during that week something inside her had simply clicked off, as if all desire and emotion for Hugh had vanished.

Perhaps it was the evening at a card shop when she hunted just the right verse for her husband. Sentimental phrases such as "For all the loving words you say" taunted her. *They're lies, they're all lies.* At last she had settled for a silly picture of Santa with a superficial rhyme, something she might give a nominal friend or the paper boy, certainly not the man she had pledged her life to.

CHAPTER 10

Then Friday night while greeting her husband, Audra confronted a strange new void. Gone were the heart flutters and the eagerness to see him. His embrace meant nothing, and she felt clad in iron. Shuddering at the remembrance, she quipped, "I've turned into a human armadillo."

Oddly, though, she didn't feel pain either. Hugh's indifference didn't seem to hurt her anymore. And on Sunday evening when she headed back to the interstate, back to Nashville, she numbly went her way without the usual sorrow tugging at her.

That week she heard from Craig McGregor twice. "So you don't think much of chapter 6, and you want to crop out—how much?" he wrote. "Please give serious consideration to the revision I've submitted. I think you'll find it more in keeping with your theology." Then he went on to say:

> You're probably correct, however, about the pantheism. After all, I've always loved scrub oak groves and suspect the love of trees is deeply buried in the marrow of us Anglo-Saxons. 'Tis true, Christianity provides my salvation, but older things lurk in me genetically (like tenderness toward wee crawlies). My soul responds not to drums or bells, but to faraway melodic piping. I believe strongly in the Christian message, but I also feel the ancient magic of trees and wood and stone and lonely moors with night whispering among the branches.

Audra shook her head. "It still sounds pagan to me."

The editing of McGregor's manuscript was proceeding more slowly than Audra had anticipated. She couldn't seem to find enough large blocks of time to concentrate on it and determined to make it a priority right after Christmas.

Then Craig's next letter took up where the previous one had ended:

> I've never felt so contented saying my prayers, as when I lay prostrate with my nose in the dew of the forest ground,

THE TEMPTING OF AUDRA GREY

surrounded by old trees and hearing a stream fighting rocks off in the distance.

Then Craig apologized for taking up her valuable time. He hoped, though, she might be able to incorporate some of his "prattle" into the text of the manuscript.

Audra smiled, admitting to herself that she rather enjoyed his prattling. It refreshed her to learn more about this man who seemed unencumbered by the trappings of materialism. At the same time, she wondered if he was encumbered by an almost occult affection for nature. But then she remembered that he had been orphaned and had been brought up by various relatives, "which was good," Craig had told her. He explained, "They each taught me something different. And I also learned to retreat to the hills and hollows for comfort. While others felt the need for people, I found a refuge in the beauty around me. Perhaps God was preparing me then for this life of bachelorhood."

About a week before Christmas, arctic air muscled its way down into Tennessee and sent thermometers plummeting. Shivering through the dark on her way to the neighborhood Bible study, Audra thought about Hugh's "frost" that had pervaded their home and how her own heart had numbed toward him recently.

"Perhaps I'll die young," she mused, "and when the medical students do an autopsy, they'll gaze aghast upon my shriveled-up innards and mutter among themselves, "'Twas the cold, for sure, that got her—freeze-dried!'"

"Oh, no!" Audra huffed at the night. "I'm beginning to sound like Craig McGregor!"

The next morning, ice glazed her window. "Fourteen degrees!" she murmured as she scowled at the thermometer fastened outside.

Her car didn't appreciate the cold either, because it coughed and grumbled before starting. Later when it hummed along the road to work, Audra found herself admiring scenes that only winter could paint. Every twig and tree and rooftop had suddenly turned silver with the sunrise.

CHAPTER 10

That afternoon, about a half-hour before quitting time, she heard Craig McGregor's voice over the phone. "I'm in Nashville," he said, "delivering some sculptures to the shop."

"So you've decided to trust another flatlander?" she teased, trying to ignore the rapid beating of her heart.

"Yep, the fellow's OK. Maybe I've been a bigot," he confessed. "Anyway, I've rewritten another portion of my manuscript and wondered if you'd have time to look at it."

"Where are you?" she asked.

"Downtown Nashville."

"You'll never make it through traffic before we close," Audra said. "Will you drive back home tonight?"

"Actually, I'm flying most of the way. A pilot friend of mine and I did some bartering so I could catch a ride over here with my little wooden creatures." Craig then suggested, "You're not too far from the airport. Would you mind meeting me there for a spell? I'm not sure when John will be able to take off again. So I need to set myself down in the lobby someplace and wait for him to show up."

Between the thudding of her heart and the clamoring of her conscience, Audra's mind was spinning. She had promised herself never to meet this man again outside the workplace, and here she was glibly replying, "All right! How about meeting me over by the American Airlines ticket section?"

Audra preached to herself all the way to the airport's short-term parking lot. She needed to act businesslike, to keep in mind a positive witness for her Lord—no matter that her stomach churned and her heart raced every time she met Craig McGregor. She had no control over that. But she could control her voice and actions. "Help me, Lord—please!" she prayed.

Stepping through the automatic doors into Nashville's international airport, Audra faced a three-dimensional "Y" of escalators, five of them linking three stories—a cascade of chrome and glass. In spite of the modern decor, the airport's spaciousness and its soft hues of sage green were as friendly and warm as a true Southern welcome.

Taking one escalator, Audra left the rental-car section behind and glided upward toward the baggage-claim area. She then boarded another escalator. It seemed that as she rose higher, so did the pitch of excitement stirring within her.

By the time she spotted Craig, her stomach had twisted into a tight knot. Still, her greeting to him sounded breezy and confident.

"I've brought you a little Christmas present," he replied, pulling an object from the pocket of his heavy woolen jacket. In the giant hand rested a small sculpted bird, a sparrow so exquisitely detailed it looked as if it might fly away.

In that instant Audra forgot her resolve and squealed with delight. "Oh, it's adorable. Thank you!" Then she quickly recovered her composure and glanced around through the bustling throng of holiday travelers. "Is there someplace we might sit where I can read your revision?" she asked primly.

He flashed her a grin, motioning, "Over here!" She followed him to a maroon couch with just the right amount of space left for the two of them.

Taking up the manuscript, Audra recalled briefly the image of the sculpted sparrow resting in Craig's hand. "How can fingers so huge carve an image in such detail?" she wondered and was tempted to ask, then dismissed the notion at once. She must be businesslike and a positive witness for the Lord. She must not allow herself to stray from the purpose of the visit.

Untouched by the confusion and noise around her, Audra sank back into McGregor's world along the Blue Ridge. She read intently and, at last, looked up through a blur of tears. "This is perfect," she murmured. "I'll hardly have to change a thing. Thank you!"

They lingered there on the maroon couch among tall potted plants and talked as if they had known each other a lifetime. A festive, easy spirit permeated the place, where children flitted among bulging pieces of luggage and doting adults. Through the hubbub, relaxed drawls from an elderly couple floated to Audra. She glanced over at them—a tall, white-haired gentleman clasping the hand of a shorter, plump woman, her lacquered hairdo fresh from a beauty shop. The twosome looked as starry-eyed and eager as honeymooners a half-century younger. And at the sight of them, a slight pain twinged in Audra's heart.

CHAPTER 10

She turned back to the bearded man beside her. He resembled a youthful version of Santa Claus in his red plaid jacket, loose-fitting slacks, and black boots. There was even a magic twinkle in his pale blue eyes.

Magic. Perhaps Craig McGregor was in reality a secret sorcerer sent by Satan himself to snag her from the "straight and narrow."

"But how could someone so caring and sensitive be of the devil?" she argued silently. In fact, Craig had a brightness about him, a special knack for cheering not only her, but probably anyone he came in contact with.

In that moment she flinched at his words: "I'm glad to see you laugh so much this evening, Miz Audra. Maybe God has sent me into your life to help you not be so serious."

Audra wondered if the opposite were true. But she said lightly, "Oh, I'm not that serious—only with my authors. I have to keep them in their place, you know."

Craig gazed beyond her and suddenly called softly, "John! I'd like you to meet my editor-friend, Miz Audra Grey."

She stood to shake the pilot's hand. "I'm pleased to meet you." John nodded politely, but looked troubled. "The weather may keep us grounded tonight. I'm not sure, McGregor. I hope you don't mind sleeping here in the lobby if need be."

Craig chuckled. "I wouldn't mind. But I think my relatives could probably take us home. They're real hospitable folks."

Feeling intrusive, Audra began to pull on her gloves.

"You're not leaving already, are you?" Craig asked.

"I should get back to my apartment before the roads turn too icy," she said.

John excused himself and left the couple facing each other in the center of the concourse. Craig's admiration for her showed openly when he declared, "I really appreciate your coming over here, Miz Audra, and I'm glad you like what I wrote."

He searched her eyes with such intensity that she couldn't speak. She felt locked in an uncertain silence with a hundred unspoken questions darting between them. Then abruptly she shut her eyes, as if breaking the spell he held over her.

"Thank you again for the sparrow," she uttered lamely. "I'll keep it on my desk."

THE TEMPTING OF AUDRA GREY

He took her hand in both of his and squeezed it gently. "I hope you and your family have a very merry Christmas," he said.

"Goodbye, Craig!" She noticed he was still holding her hand, and she wasn't pulling away. She liked being with this giant-sized man whose every word was a celebration of life. "You have a blessed Christmas yourself up in those snowy mountains!"

She withdrew slowly and walked in a daze toward the escalator. *What's happening to me? Am I losing my mind? Worse yet, am I losing my experience with the Lord?* Before she reached the parking lot, Audra vowed, "I must phone Julie."

Chapter 11

Afternoon sunlight reflected off clustered icicles, transforming the freeway's ordinary rocky banks into a dazzling display of multicolored prisms. "Nature's own Christmas ornaments," Audra breathed, glad that the publishing house had closed early. Now she could return to Knoxville before the soft fluff of snow, which powdered the countryside, turned treacherous.

She concentrated on the music that swelled inside her car, on the beauty of chilled and distant mountains, on anything that might dim the memory that haunted her. She could see him plainly, Craig McGregor, his red plaid jacket stretched over his strong torso, the pale eyes. And what had she read in those eyes—simple admiration or something more?

"I mustn't think of him," she murmured, reminding herself, "I'm a Christian, a married woman."

Then a faint smile crossed her lips. How fitting that the Sunday school lesson that week covered the seventh chapter of Romans. She would tell her class how Paul had felt like a split personality when he wrote in verse 10—"What I do is not the good I want to do; no, the evil I do not want to do—this I keep on doing" (NIV). Something akin to a civil war raged inside him, the same kind of war that raged inside Audra at the moment, her spiritual nature at odds with the carnal. But she wouldn't dare confess that to her class. After all, she had an image to uphold—Mrs. Audra Grey, devoted wife and mother, pillar of the church and community. Such a confession would only hurt people, create a "stumbling block" for the weaker ones. No, she decided,

THE TEMPTING OF AUDRA GREY

some problems were best left exclusively between God and the struggling person.

Then she whispered, "Please, Father, help me to get through this without letting go of my hold on You."

Some relief followed while she listened to a sermon on the Twenty-third Psalm. At first Audra was tempted to switch stations. What new could a minister say about this familiar portion of Scripture anyway? But the psalm was examined through the eyes of an ancient sheepherder, each section explained in light of the shepherd's precise duties to his flock.

The radio minister began by reading the first verse, then commenting, "Safely in the fold at night, the sheep don't fret about their grazing the next day. They trust the shepherd, even if he takes them back over the same grazing ground." The voice chuckled, asking, "Has the Lord been guiding you over some of the same grazing ground lately?"

"As a matter of fact," Audra replied saucily, "I feel as if I've been stuck in the same grazing ground for a couple of decades now." Then she realized she hadn't actually noticed "the sparseness of the grass" until after both her children had left for college. That was when she and Hugh had begun living apart.

The minister led his listeners through the rest of the verses. And when the half-hour segment ended, Audra felt as soothed as one of the sheep in the Shepherd Psalm. It was as if God Himself had slipped a private message to her over the airwaves, "Don't worry, Audra! You're important to Me. I love you. I'll get you safely through this deep valley." Her heart stirred with thankfulness as the car weaved its last miles toward her hillside home.

Dusk had thickened, and an evening hush had settled over the neighborhood when Audra arrived. Even the dog seemed subdued. But a whirlwind awaited on the other side of the door. Andy was first to hug her, whisking off with her bags. Then Natalie kissed her cheek soundly while bubbling, "Merry Christmas!"

"Merry Christmas!" Audra sang out, competing with carols blaring from the stereo. She took in the strong evergreen scent hanging in the air and the tree, glittering in the picture window. Underneath it sprawled her husband, who was tinkering with a string of lights.

CHAPTER 11

"I'm home!" she called to him.

"That's nice," he said.

Audra was suddenly seized with an impulse to retort, "And a bah-humbug to you too!" Instead, she wandered over to him and said, "Hugh, this is Julie's first Christmas since the divorce. She must be feeling pretty lonely. Would you mind if I phoned her?"

He rolled over and looked up, a wry expression on his handsome face. "You two have never been able to talk without the conversation lasting at least an hour."

Audra giggled, admitting, "You're right. But could you consider it an extra Christmas gift to me?"

He rose to his feet and shrugged. "I don't care."

Audra waited until her husband drove the children to the mall. Then she dialed the number in Michigan.

As soon as she heard the familiar, "Hello," words came gushing forth. "Julie! How good to hear your voice! I was thinking, this is your first Christmas without Bill. How are you handling it?"

"It's good to hear you too. And to be honest, I'm kind of riding a roller coaster of emotions right now," Julie confided. "But I've got a wonderful Christian counselor who's helping me a lot. Oh, Audra! I had no idea how much I've depended upon people and work for my self-esteem instead of upon God."

"Really?" That was hard for Audra to believe. Julie was one of the most spiritual persons she knew.

"I've learned so much," her friend said, "and I've got a lot more to learn." Then Julie turned her attention to Audra. "Tell me, how are you doing?"

Audra hesitated, then decided to charge ahead. "Well, if it's honesty you want, then I think I'm going crazy."

Julie laughed only a moment before her voice abruptly filled with concern. "You're not joking, are you."

Audra's lips quivered as she opened up to her friend. She told about Hugh's preoccupation with his job, about his ignoring her, about what she termed her "sham of a marriage," about her profound loneliness in Nashville, and even about her unwanted feelings for Craig McGregor. "I don't know what's happening to me, Julie. I've never faced anything like this before. How can I push Craig out of my thoughts? I feel so ugly and rotten."

THE TEMPTING OF AUDRA GREY

"Audra, dear, I think you've confused temptation with sin. They are two different animals, you know."

"Yes, but it's getting harder to tell the difference."

"God made us with feelings," Julie insisted. "You can't help how you respond emotionally to Craig. But you can tell God all about it—exactly how you feel. Describe the temptations to Him, everything!"

Audra gasped. "But, Julie, my thoughts sometimes border on the lustful. God is pure and good. He can't stand sin."

"But He loves you, Audra, and He loves honesty," Julie said. "You've got to learn to trust Him with your very personal feelings. Anyway," she declared, "my psychologist tells me that when I voice my troubles aloud, it causes at least some of my anxiety to dissipate."

"Well, I suppose I could give it a try."

Then her friend surprised Audra: "I was wondering when all the years of stuffing away your hurt and frustration would finally catch up with you."

"What do you mean?"

"I mean, Audra, that you're a nurturer. Because I'm a nurturer too, I can talk openly to you. We're the do-gooder people, the holder-uppers, the ones who counsel others, help people through various tragedies, pray with them and for them. But tell me, Audra, when was the last time you actually nurtured yourself?"

"Well, let's see—I study my Bible and journal and pray each morning, and I walk at least two miles a day, and—"

Julie interrupted her. "Those might be considered nurturing. But when was the last time you actually hugged yourself by luxuriating in a hot bubble bath or by treating yourself to supper at a restaurant or by splurging on a concert?"

"Hugh and I don't go out much," Audra replied. "We've been on a really tight budget."

"I don't mean you and Hugh. I mean you—all by yourself!"

Audra frowned. "That sounds sort of selfish, don't you think?"

"Ah-ha! I knew it. See? Nurturing types like us feel guilty if we do something special for our own selves."

"But that doesn't sound at all Christian," Audra argued.

"Stop and think about this: Jesus commanded, 'Love your neighbor as yourself.' Doesn't that mean that God expects us to

CHAPTER 11

love ourselves in the first place? And shouldn't that love be the same kind of nurturing love that you give others?"

"Well, I don't know." Audra hesitated, uncomfortable with this turn in the conversation. She was beginning to harbor serious doubts about her friend's psychologist and his Christian experience.

"Would you do me a favor?" Julie pleaded. "Would you at least start a bit of nurturing? It doesn't have to be something big and expensive, just a bubble bath by candlelight with beautiful symphony music playing on your stereo."

"Yes, that shouldn't hurt anything," Audra agreed. "And you know, when I think about it, this phone call wasn't entirely unselfish," she confessed. "I just had to talk to you, Julie. There's no one in either Knoxville or Nashville that I can share my deepest feelings with—no one," she repeated. "I miss you terribly."

"And I miss you. You know, Audra, people view you as the perfect mother, the perfect wife, the perfect church member. If you'd just quit playing games and level with a few of the trustworthy ones, let them know you're a fallible person, ask for their prayers, then maybe that would help not only you, but them as well." Julie paused before proceeding, "I don't want you to feel insulted, Audra, but sometimes you're so good you're intimidating. Maybe the Lord has allowed this McGregor fellow into your life simply to help you come down off that pedestal of yours and to become more human."

"More human?" Audra repeated in exasperation. "But aren't we supposed to strive for more Christlike characters as we grow in Him?"

"Yes, but what is Christlike? I think it's being truthful, taking off our masks, getting in touch with life and the beauty all around us—and in touch with our real feelings."

Audra cringed. "Now you're beginning to sound like my mountain friend," she said.

"Well, maybe he's more of a Christian than either one of us, then."

"Hmmm! I don't know. I feel terribly confused, Julie."

"I'm sorry. But, Audra, you've got to admit you're rarely genuine with people. Most of your relationships are one-sided.

THE TEMPTING OF AUDRA GREY

You minister to others, but what do they give back?"

"Oh, I get something in return—warm, fuzzy feelings."

Julie continued to hammer her point. "But, admit it, most of your relationships with people aren't two-sided. Even your marriage, which is especially important to you, is mostly give."

"That's not entirely true," Audra protested. "Hugh's a good provider and an excellent father."

"But people need intense personal sharing, Audra. You and your husband don't even argue. You're like married singles, trapped in two separate circles that overlap only occasionally." Then Julie reminded her friend of the recent divorce. "Divorce is a sampling of hell itself," she said sadly. "And I don't want to see my dearest friend suffer as I—"

"Julie!" Audra exclaimed. "I wouldn't even consider getting a divorce. Anyway, there'd be no biblical grounds. Hugh'll always be faithful."

"Well, that's a whole 'nuther subject," her friend drawled, "and we won't take time tonight to get into it." Then Julie's voice took on a gentler tone. "Audra, you're a strong woman. Could your fear of becoming vulnerable somehow discourage Hugh from opening up and acting like a husband should?"

"I don't know. Just the other day I was considering that my personality might overwhelm him. Perhaps that's part of the problem."

Audra could hear a smile in Julie's voice. "Do you realize you're just as much a workaholic as your husband? You also mask your feelings with work—anesthetizing yourself, if you please—the same as Hugh."

"I disagree," Audra retorted. "I try to balance my life with worship times and exercise and proper nutrition and—"

"Yes, still as organized as ever, I hear! And still spread out in a hundred different directions with your work, your Bible studies, your Sunday school teaching, your housekeeping." Julie grabbed a breath, then continued, "Someplace, Audra, under all that organization, under all that doing, is a very lonely woman."

A long silence stood between them until Audra conceded, "You're right."

CHAPTER 11

But Julie wasn't finished yet. "And you've been covering up your hurts and frustrations with all that doing for so long that I'm afraid something's going to explode pretty soon."

"In what way?"

Julie's voice sounded grim. "A person can only take so much stress until depression sets in."

The words struck Audra hard. "I'm afraid it already has."

"Have you recognized some symptoms?"

"I sometimes wake up crying for no reason; although I'm exhausted, I often have trouble sleeping; and more frequently now I feel like there's this big, black, oppressive cloud hovering over me, and nothing I do—not even prayer—can chase that oppressive feeling away." Then she forced out, "And, worst of all, I've suddenly lost any romantic feelings for Hugh. It's scary, Julie, really scary."

"Uh-oh! Audra, you need to find a good counselor like I have. Ask the pastor for a list."

"I can't share this with Pastor Jim. I can't."

"There you go again—nurturing," Julie chided. "You're protecting him from the pain of discovering the truth about your marriage."

"You're probably right, but at this stage in my life I cannot share this with my minister." In that moment Audra remembered a weekend marriage seminar that was scheduled for February. "My church in Nashville is holding a seminar as a prelude to Valentine's Day. Maybe I could get some names of good counselors there."

Julie laughed lightly. "You're not dragging Hugh off to another marriage seminar? How many will that make?"

"I've lost count," Audra chortled, feeling her mood traveling upward again.

"And are you still buying every book on marriage ever printed?"

"My shelves are bursting with them," Audra confessed lamely. "Anyway, the cost of a counselor would never fit into our budget with the kids in school."

The other woman sounded distraught, sputtering, "Then, tell me, what good will it do to have two highly educated children if their mother is either in a mental hospital or has run off to the mountains with some artist?"

"Julie! I'd never do such a thing."

"Maybe not now, my friend. But when the pressure is turned up so high that you break—" Her words trailed off into another long silence, then, "I don't want to see you lose your family—and your faith."

"But God's promised He won't allow me to suffer more than I can handle."

"Yes," Julie chirped, "and that's why He's made me your friend, so I can warn you and beg you to get professional help. Promise me you will!"

Audra hesitated. "I don't know how we'd ever swing it financially, but OK, I promise."

Just minutes after she hung up, the phone rang.

"Audra, this is Julie again."

"What did you forget?"

"Was I too hard on you tonight—too blunt, I mean? You certainly don't need more hurt right now."

"Oh, Julie!" Audra brimmed with gratitude. "You have no idea how much you've helped me. Just being able to talk to someone about my predicament has made me feel worlds lighter."

Julie made some quiet sounds of relief.

Then Audra said, "I hope, in spite of everything, you can still glean a blessing from this Christmas."

"You too, my friend! You too!"

Chapter 12

Audra stared moodily out at rain-washed hills. For her, the interstate between Knoxville and Nashville had become a place for meditating.

Scenes from Christmas replayed in her mind: Natalie giggling and tearing at packages like a two-year-old out of control; Andy, more dignified, patiently unwrapping his gifts, then folding the paper into neat stacks. Most of the scenes were happy ones staged at her in-laws' cozy farmhouse.

And for a brief moment Audra's heart had come alive again when she opened her card from Hugh. It was large and lacy, with delicate gold print. The words seemed to swirl off the page and caress her numb spirit, assuring Audra of her husband's love, his caring and need for her.

Close to tears, she choked, "Oh, honey! This is beautiful."

He responded by joking to the relatives, "I picked that up at the last minute, the only card left in the wife section."

There was a moment of brittle silence in which no one looked directly at anybody. Hugh might as well have used the card to slap Audra's face. *That's what I get for being vulnerable again.* Then she reminded herself, "No feel—no pain!"

With the new year, Audra set aside a couple of hours each workday to edit Craig McGregor's manuscript. Her goal was to have it ready for typesetting before the end of March.

"I wish he owned a phone," she complained more than once to the computer screen. "Telephoning would make this job much

THE TEMPTING OF AUDRA GREY

easier." Instead, she would accumulate a pageful of questions, then mail them off to Blowing Rock. The following week the answers would return. And Craig never failed to add a personal postscript, sharing some special insight.

> I spent Christmas with my clan down in a "holler," the snow risin' all around. . . .
> I noticed something oddly different this year. My Eddie-Mae memories that appear like unwanted ghosts at holiday times, that tug at my tender heart—they had faded just as surely as ancient photos in an album left open too long in the sun.
> I wonder, could my writing the book have brought this about?

As the weeks rolled on and temperatures moderated in the first promises of a waiting spring, Audra found her mind straying more and more to the mountain man. She anticipated his letters, his skillful, soothing words, his gentle teasing. And as the folder of his letters thickened, so did her guilt.

"Hugh," she ventured one Saturday night, "you and I need a tryst."

"A what?"

"A special time together."

"If it costs money, forget it," he grumbled.

"Actually, it wouldn't cost us much, because we can use my apartment instead of booking a motel room."

"For what?" he asked.

"A marriage seminar at my Nashville church." Before her husband could object, she hastily appealed to his innate frugality. "Just think! Staying in my apartment would mean we'd get more of our money's worth on the rent. You'd simply drive over to Nashville that weekend instead of my coming home."

Hugh wore a thoughtful frown. "You mean, I'd have to leave work early?"

"Not too early," she replied. "Remember, you gain an hour going west."

CHAPTER 12

"I don't know," he murmured.

"It'll be Valentine's Day."

After more coaxing, Hugh gave in to the idea.

Feeling giddy over the small victory, Audra looked forward to learning how to communicate better with her mate, how to convey her discontent about their living situation.

Friday of the seminar, she took off work early, sped home, showered, and recurled her hair. Although spring hadn't arrived yet, she wore a lightweight floral dress that draped flatteringly about her figure. Then she dabbed a favorite musky scent at her throat and wrists.

"All right, Hugh Grey!" she declared to the hopeful image in her mirror, "try ignoring me now!"

He did. In fact, he made a perfect picture of boredom throughout the meetings. And instead of filling in the worksheets, he marked up the margins with meaningless doodles.

Still, Audra remained undaunted and used their "communication skills practice" to convey her feelings about their living apart. For her every plea, however, Hugh tossed back a strong rebuttal.

"Andy'll be going directly into medical school when he graduates," her husband pointed out. "And Natalie still has two years left in college. How could you even think of quitting such a high-paying job at this critical time in their lives?"

"What about *our* lives, Hugh? We keep putting us on hold until some nebulous future date." She reached over and patted his hand. "We're not getting any younger, honey. I'd like the years we have left to be full and meaningful."

"I find it quite meaningful to help our children toward good careers so they don't have to struggle as we did."

"But sometimes struggle draws us closer to God," she contended gently. "And it makes us more responsible. Anyway, other kids get student loans—"

"And other kids spend years paying back those loans, never having enough to save for a down payment on a house."

Audra gave up. She had to admit that Hugh's reasoning was sound. And she, too, wanted to help their children become successful adults. "Maybe I'm being selfish," she considered, wandering off in search of a drinking fountain. Then, incon-

THE TEMPTING OF AUDRA GREY

spicuously, she approached one of the guest speakers and asked for the name of a Christian counselor in Knoxville.

"There are several," he said, taking out his own business card and writing on the reverse side.

She slid the card into her pocket, feeling deceptive for acting behind her husband's back. *But Hugh would never understand.*

Later that Sunday afternoon, with a forced smile and wave, Audra sent Hugh on his journey back to Knoxville. She breathed deeply of the cooling air, noting a nameless yearning within her. Then she recognized it as a yearning for intimacy with her husband, with her children, with her friends, and especially with God. She wondered whether every person on earth also craves this same intimacy. Was this the craving that drives the human race in unending circles?

She sighed again, realizing she had placed too much hope on the marriage seminar, expecting a miracle cure in one weekend. She gazed up the slope where the same medieval towers stood. But now they brooded, looking sad in that uncertain time between winter and spring.

She pulled the card from her pocket and squinted at the name listed first—Dr. Kelchner. "I'll phone tomorrow," she decided, "and see whether I can make an appointment for the weekend."

That night she tossed sleeplessly for hours. The oppressive cloud had returned, the loneliness heavy upon her like a leaden blanket. *I shouldn't have gotten my hopes up. I shouldn't have.* She had tried to impress her husband, wanting him to notice her, to open up, to offer her one small sign of love. But Hugh had remained his same stolid, closed self.

Then her mind would vault to another man so different from her spouse. She kept pushing the image of Craig McGregor aside. But a jumble of recollections crowded in on her: the blue eyes brimful of warmth and caring, the muscular man leaning against a column near the Greek warrior at the capitol grounds. Then she compared Craig's heavily muscled arms with those of the statue, and she wondered for one fleeting moment how it would feel to be enfolded by those arms.

In that instant she prayed, "Help me not to think of Craig that way, Lord! Help me to keep him in the proper perspective as a

CHAPTER 12

client and friend." She felt caught between two powerful forces that long night, and slept little.

Her study the next morning focused on 1 Peter 1:13: "Gird up the loins of your mind, be sober, and hope to the end for the grace that is to be brought unto you at the revelation of Jesus Christ."

In her journal, she related that Scripture passage to her life:

> If I could simply keep "the loins of my mind" girded up at all times, I would have much greater victory over sin. It's my thoughts that defeat me spiritually.
>
> I think God Himself has to be the "girder upper," though, because only through the power of the Holy Spirit can my mind be free from these tempting thoughts. I know I can't do it by myself. I've tried again and again, but I'm powerless.

Audra closed the journal. She had considered herself fully committed to Christ and His will for her life. She was supposed to be filled with the Holy Spirit. "But how can I be filled with the Spirit and, at the same time, be attracted to a man who's not my husband?"

Yes, today she would phone for an appointment. She must see Dr. Kelchner as quickly as possible.

Chapter 13

The psychologist's waiting room was modest, with the usual outdated magazines and ailing plants. Audra sat in a corner, thumbing nervously through one of the journals. This was her first experience with a counselor, and her anxiety had become almost unbearable.

A few minutes later the receptionist led Audra down a narrow corridor to a smaller room, where a lean man looked up at her through dark-rimmed glasses. He had a pleasant face with a high forehead and inquisitive, bright eyes. "I'm Dr. Kelchner," he announced, rising to shake her hand, then settling again behind his desk. His manner gave the impression of wisdom and experience.

"And I'm Audra Grey," she returned in a shaky voice.

"Please, sit down! May I call you Audra?"

She nodded as she sank into the upholstered chair across from him. "My husband doesn't even know I'm here," she said. "But I felt I needed to talk with someone before I go bananas or something."

With an amused expression, he asked, "Why don't you tell me why you think you might, as you said, 'go bananas'?"

At first it was hard for Audra to talk to this stranger. But she quickly found his manner nonjudgmental and sincere. In little time, she relaxed and began unburdening herself.

Before mentioning Craig McGregor, however, she inquired, "Is everything I say here confidential? No one in my church or family—not even your receptionist—would ever find out?"

CHAPTER 13

"No one," he assured her.

When she finished her story, he clasped his hands together and leaned forward. "Audra, I'd like you to imagine your tempting thoughts as birds flying through a large, airy barn. They can fly through without causing concern, but when you allow them to roost and build nests there, the problems begin."

Mulling over his words, she concluded, "So you're telling me essentially what my friend, Julie, said—that my thoughts are just temptation, not sin."

"As long as you don't dwell on them and cultivate them—that is, give them a medium in which to grow—no, Audra, they're not sin."

She heard her own long sigh. "What a relief! I felt as if I had suddenly thrown out my relationship with the Lord and had become a Jezebel overnight."

"Hardly!" He chuckled. "And I'm sure God wouldn't let you go without a struggle. You're very special to Him, you know." Then the counselor removed his glasses and rubbed the bridge of his nose. "But you do have some serious problems," he declared, "especially in regard to your husband and your living apart so much. This is too dangerous a time in your lives to be separated. You need closeness more than ever, now that your children are leaving."

Without warning, her eyes began to fill. "But, doctor, I'm just as lonely when I'm with Hugh as when we're apart." She rushed on, disclosing, "I feel empty inside, but guilty for not appreciating my husband. After all, he doesn't beat me or anything. And I'm sure many women would gladly trade places with me."

Handing her a tissue, the counselor said, "Tell me, if Hugh would open up and become an affectionate husband, if he would learn to communicate with you and you with him, if you two could enjoy some fun together, do you think this other man would still seem desirable?"

Audra hesitated only a moment. "I doubt that Craig would be much of a temptation at all."

"Good! Now, how can we convince your husband to fill out these questionnaires, then come in with you to see me?"

A wry laugh escaped her. "Do you have a tranquilizer gun I could borrow?"

THE TEMPTING OF AUDRA GREY

"That difficult, huh?"

"Yes," she sadly concurred. "There's really no place in our budget for counseling right now."

"We can work with you on that," he offered. "I have an idea. Tell Hugh that in order for you to be helped, I need to talk with him. That's true, and it might bring him in—at least once. But I should evaluate his—and your—questionnaires first." The counselor smiled reassuringly. "Audra, I believe there's real hope for your marriage."

She perked up. "You do?"

"Yes. You see, many couples seek my help after one of the partners has had an affair. Then it's a lot of work to heal all that pain. But in your case you've recognized the danger signals ahead of time. If your husband is as intelligent as I think he is, he should be able to learn how to start sharing himself with you." Then the doctor asked, "Do you mind if I pray before you leave?"

"Oh, please do!" she breathed.

During his prayer, Audra could sense the weight of guilt soaring away from her, taking with it the dark cloud of depression. And when she emerged from the office into a clear, sunny day, the world looked freshly painted. And almost immediately she noticed that thoughts of Craig McGregor weren't dominating her mind anymore. Like the faded photos he had once alluded to, Craig's own image had grown fainter. Whether that image, the guilt, or the depression would return was open to question, but for now Audra felt free.

She especially appreciated what the counselor had said about comparing her tainted thoughts with birds. That advice not to let the thoughts "roost and build nests" was well worth the expense of the visit, she decided.

"Now, if I can just convince Hugh to fill out these questionnaires, then go with me to visit Dr. Kelchner—"

Chapter 14

Audra couldn't believe she was actually strolling alongside Hugh straight into Dr. Kelchner's office—or were they floating? She didn't know which of her statements had convinced her husband to fill out the questionnaires, then accompany her "at least once." But something—perhaps prayer—had worked, and there they were. The psychologist wanted to see Hugh for the first half-hour, then counsel with both of them after that.

As the minutes crept by in the vacant waiting room, Audra gazed out at the bleak afternoon, where the March wind tossed leaves and litter about the deserted parking lot. Her little car waited for her there, ready for its trip back to Nashville.

Reaching for the chapter of *Eddie Mae and Me* she had packed in her purse, Audra reviewed it with halfhearted interest. She had nearly completed the editing. Only two weeks remained before the deadline to send the manuscript to the typesetter.

"Then I won't hear from Craig anymore," she reflected, "at least not until he corrects the proofs. But that shouldn't happen for weeks yet." A sadness settled upon Audra when she considered life without Craig's whimsical insights on nature and life in general. Then her mind returned to what was occurring behind closed doors down the hall. Perhaps after today, she wouldn't need Craig's notes anymore to bolster her morale. Perhaps Dr. Kelchner held some magical key that would unlock Hugh's reserve.

Her hopes rose with every passing minute. Mingling with those hopes was gratitude for the counselor, who had made an

THE TEMPTING OF AUDRA GREY

appointment for them on a Sunday. She guessed that he viewed his work more as a ministry than as a job.

At last Dr. Kelchner's baritone called to her over the intercom, and she hurried to the other office. Despite the tired circles dragging at his eyes, the counselor greeted her with his usual enthusiasm, offering the chair beside her husband.

The look of distress written across Hugh's face wrenched Audra's heart. She suddenly felt a motherly urge to grab his hand and spirit him off, away from all the inner searchings that obviously made him uncomfortable. Then the thought struck her, "He's putting himself through this misery for me." Maybe Hugh did love her after all!

"Here are copies of the evaluations for each of you," the counselor said. "If you'll look at page 1 first, I'll explain." He settled again behind his desk and began, "This chart shows us whether you're basically introverted or extroverted. Audra, you'll notice that, for the most part, your line on the graph stays on the extreme right. That tells us that you're outgoing. You'll also observe that you rank highest in expressing your affection to others."

Audra's eyes were skipping down the other page, searching for her spouse's graph. But Hugh had already found it, because he said sheepishly, "Looks like mine is an exact opposite of hers!"

"Well, often the old adage that opposites attract is true. And that can be good," Dr. Kelchner emphasized. Then he noted, "In your work as an accountant, you don't have to be exceptionally outgoing, so your occupation pretty well fits your personality. But the inability to express affection to your wife can be very frustrating for her, I'm sure."

"Yes, we talked about that," Hugh mumbled.

"Can you tell Audra why you may have difficulty demonstrating your affection?"

Hugh looked at the floor instead of at her. "I think we decided that it has something to do with the role models in my own family. My parents hardly ever kissed or hugged in front of us children. In fact, I don't remember their showing any love to each other at all, although Mother did hug us children at times. And I don't recall any words of affection between my parents either."

CHAPTER 14

The counselor thanked him, then speculated, "Audra, I would guess that your parents were very demonstrative with their affection."

She giggled. "For everyone—each other, us kids, the neighbors, the neighbors' dog!"

Dr. Kelchner enjoyed a hearty laugh before he directed them to the individual profiles. "You'll notice that you two do share a few personality traits."

That revelation encouraged Audra. Maybe she and Hugh had something in common after all.

"Let's see. You're both intelligent, you're both very moralistic and self-controlled, with high willpower—the husband much more than the wife on that last one."

When Audra placed Hugh's graph next to hers, however, she noticed the obvious swings in opposite directions. "The rest of this looks like my husband and I don't even speak the same language," she exclaimed.

A smile still lingered on the doctor's face. "In some ways you don't. But look back up at letter B. That tells us you're both intelligent, remember? Therefore, you have the ability to bring some of these extremes more toward the center. That would ease the strain in communicating."

He rubbed his chin thoughtfully and continued, "Now, I do detect a possible hurdle here, something that can cause real trouble. Hugh, you'll notice the places I've circled where you're firmly fixed in your behavior. For instance, you're highly stable, conscientious, controlled, plus tough-minded and self-reliant. Now let's put those traits together with Audra's weaknesses." They all shifted to her chart. "Look here! She's affected by feelings, and at this time in her life she's vulnerable and emotionally less stable than you are. You'll also notice she's accommodating. That means she won't assert herself, especially if she thinks she might hurt someone's feelings in the slightest."

Audra suddenly felt as if she were sitting there not only stripped of her clothes, but of her skin as well. "Poor Hugh!" she mutely sympathized now that she was experiencing similar discomfort.

"Audra, you need to assert yourself more," Dr. Kelchner said. "Tell Hugh how you feel instead of keeping those things inside you."

THE TEMPTING OF AUDRA GREY

"I've tried. I even used word pictures—a story about a poor tree that shrivels up and dies—but it worked for only a few minutes."

The doctor shook his head. "Remember, both of you, it's taken years to form these behavior patterns. You can't alter them overnight. In fact, you might not be able to change them at all—just bring them more to the center."

Then he addressed Hugh. "Could you tell your wife what you've decided needs to be done?"

Hugh again looked so ill at ease that Audra cringed. She hated to see him suffer.

"Well," her husband began, looking down at his shoes, "I should probably try to show her more how I feel and tell her I love her and things like that."

"Yes, and what about your living apart? What did we decide there?"

Hugh relaxed a little. Audra recalled how much easier he could talk about facts than about feelings.

"You said it was dangerous for us to be living apart."

"So do either of you have ideas about how to change that situation?"

Audra piped up, "I could start looking for a job in Knoxville, maybe a part-time teaching position at a college, like I had before."

"Yeah," Hugh said, "but you wouldn't make the kind of money you're making now."

"And would that be so bad?" the doctor asked.

"It would mean we couldn't keep both our kids in school," Hugh said flatly. "There's no way I can take on more clients, either. I've got too many already and have to work overtime as it is."

"But you like your work, don't you?" the doctor persisted.

"For the most part," Hugh said, looking pleased.

Their hour was up, and when the couple rose to leave, Audra thanked Dr. Kelchner. "Just seeing our personalities in black and white has helped me immensely. And I really appreciate your meeting with us on a Sunday."

"No problem," the counselor told her. "And if you both would like to come back on a regular basis for a while, I'd be delighted to meet with you whenever we can fit the sessions into your busy schedules."

CHAPTER 14

Audra thanked him again, and Hugh echoed her, but with less enthusiasm.

The couple wandered out to the lot, where their cars sat side by side. The wind, catching at Audra's skirt, also rearranged her husband's blond locks, whipping them down on his forehead.

His disheveled, little-boy look made her heart skip lightly. "So what did you think?" she asked.

"It was OK."

"Then would you mind if I at least started looking for a new job here in Knoxville?"

"Do what you want."

"What about coming back to see Dr. Kelchner again? Do you think we could manage to squeeze the expense into our budget for a month or so?" She could hear the hope rising in her voice.

"Audra, it would be a waste of money. I don't plan to change."

His words poured over her like ice water. "What?" she asked incredulously.

"I said, I don't plan to change. I am who I am. And if you don't like that, well then, I'm sorry."

A swirling in Audra's head forced her to lean against the car. "But, Hugh," her voice trembled. "I don't want you to change. I just want you to reach deep down within yourself and pull up the caring, affectionate man I know is under there someplace. I've seen him interact with the children and our pets. Is it so selfish of me to want that affection too?"

Her husband glanced at his watch. "It's growing late. Hadn't you better get on the road?"

After her impassioned plea, his response—cold and heartless—rattled inside her like a heavy chain, bruising everything it touched.

"You're right. I'd better get on the road."

She considered trying to bully Hugh into therapy. She could say, "OK, then, I want a divorce!" or "Maybe I'll just have an affair—"

With a stab of honesty, Audra admitted to herself, "Dr. Kelchner was right. I despise confronting my husband, especially if that confrontation would hurt him." She also reminded herself that Hugh would see straight through her bluff in an instant.

THE TEMPTING OF AUDRA GREY

Therefore, she simply stood on tiptoe and kissed him goodbye, then climbed into her car. Hugh pulled out of the parking lot and into traffic veering east.

Still sitting in the parking lot, Audra let her pent-up tears flow. She might as well have burned a hundred-dollar bill back in Dr. Kelchner's office for all the good the session did, she thought.

Clouds scudded across the darkening sky before her. And any hope she had salvaged was darkening too. Audra saw herself drifting like the clouds, drifting through the endless days ahead, a prisoner marking time in a cell of her own choosing.

"And why should I look for a job here anyway?" she asked the silence. "I would be just as lonely no matter where I live." She sighed, concluding, "I guess it's better to be lonely and make more money than to be lonely and make less money." Audra pulled into the street and headed west. Still, she might at least look into possible teaching positions opening in the fall.

Chapter 15

A hush settled over Nashville and its surrounding browns and grays—that lull just before spring when gentle rains drift across Southern cities and wash away winter. Although some dawns came wrapped in cotton-thick fog, Audra could still sense the earth about to burst with new grass and flowers and rich, loamy fragrances.

Peering out her office window at a sullen drizzle, she noticed tiny buds peppering the few trees there. "Winter's lasted forever this year," she mused, and she longed for the rebirth of color. Then she posed a serious question to herself, "But would I appreciate spring so much if there were no winter?" She wondered even further if she would appreciate the personalities of people like Julie and Craig if there were no Hughs in the world. Smiling wryly, she breathed, "My poor husband! Now I'm comparing him with long, barren months."

At that moment Marie's voice came over the intercom. "Craig McGregor on line one."

How banal the "Good morning, Craig!" sounded when Audra's conscience was already sparring with fluttery feelings.

"Hi, beautiful lady!" came the slow, resonant voice that sometimes tracked through her dreams. "What're ya doing?"

"As a matter of fact, I'm working on a speech."

"A speech for what?"

"A writer's conference in Tacoma, Washington, this summer," she answered. "A university requested that our publishing house send an editor to teach a few classes, interview writers, things like that. And I was elected for the job."

THE TEMPTING OF AUDRA GREY

"Lucky you!" he declared. "Washington's an incredibly beautiful state. You'll have to take time out to visit Mount Rainier, maybe cruise across the sound, and even drive over to the coast. The Pacific Ocean is different from the Atlantic, you know."

She laughed. "I didn't realize that. But I'm sure, if there are any differences, you would detect them."

Background noises, typical around a telephone booth, whirred and rumbled over the line while Craig apologized for disturbing her at work. "But I just mailed the final corrections back to you," he said, "and the more I consider not hearing from you anymore, the bleaker my future looks."

"Craig—"

"Please, hear me out!" he interrupted. "Would you mind if I simply wrote a note to you once a week, describing a sunrise or the birthing of seasons up here in the mountains? Nothing fancy or amorous, I promise. Then would you kindly share your reactions and maybe add a report of your own?"

"But my part in producing your book is finished for several months," she protested. "How would such letters look to my secretary?"

"We could use your home address in Nashville," he suggested.

While she groped for an appropriate reply, Audra's conscience prodded, *This is wrong. He's a man—and not your husband.* Finally, she said, "If you were a woman, Craig, I wouldn't hesitate to keep up our correspondence. You see, because my life is so stressful, with work and all the projects I'm involved in, your letters always refresh me. Reading them is like dangling my feet in a cool stream on a hot summer's day and—" She caught herself speaking in a "McGregorism" again and finished abruptly. "I wouldn't feel comfortable, however, corresponding with you outside the workplace."

His tone turned sober. "Don't you trust me?"

"It's not a matter of trustworthiness, Craig, but a matter of propriety."

"Ah! Miz Audra Pureheart again—prim, proper, and prudish." Then he chuckled softly. "And pompous, perhaps?"

"Excellent alliteration!" she declared, feeling some of the tension drain away. "I don't mean to sound pompous," she

CHAPTER 15

defended herself. "It's just that I really value my witness as a Christian and how other people perceive me."

Craig wouldn't be dismissed that easily. "And who's to know I'm writing you at home?" Then he answered his own question. "The letter carrier maybe. And he's probably never set eyes on you. Anyway, what difference does it make? We're kindred spirits, Audra. We're both creative types. You're more perceptive than any of my other artist friends." He sighed wearily, and sadness crept into his voice. "I've finally found someone who loves to hear me rattle on about rivers wriggling and streams dribbling, and now your silly propriety wants to end our friendship just because I'm a man. That sounds kind of bigoted, don't you think?"

Audra's conscience wrestled with the ramifications of allowing this charming man to become even more entwined with her life. "Craig, listen, I don't want to end our friendship. I really do appreciate your right-brained ways. In fact, I find them delightful. But my conservative faith has never had to deal with anyone like you before." Then an idea struck her. "I'll tell you what. Next weekend I'll simply ask my husband for his advice, what he thinks about my corresponding with you."

"Sounds fair!" Craig said without hesitating. "Meanwhile," he added, "take good care of yourself, sweet lady! I worry about your living all alone in that big city."

She again felt heartened by his concern. "I'm not alone, remember?"

"Oh, yeah!" He laughed. "I nearly forgot about those angels of yours, the ones who might know karate!"

"Yes, those angels," she repeated, reliving briefly the walk around the capitol grounds. "Goodbye, Mr. McGregor!"

"Goodbye, Mrs. Grey!"

Audra put down the phone and exhaled deeply. "OK, Hugh," she whispered, "Dr. Kelchner said you were the sensible one of us, that I depend too much on my feelings to make decisions. So now's your chance to tell me what to do."

Palm Sunday was brightened by tulips waking in flower beds along the road home from church. The clear, cloudless sky and warming air brought some peace to Audra's chaotic world. Letting contentment flow through her, she thought of her children returning soon for Easter and her parents traveling from Hickory for the holiday as well.

She grinned at the prospect and also at the absurdity of asking her husband's permission to write another man. Still, she decided to broach the subject. "Hugh, there's this author-friend of mine. He's also a sculptor and teacher. He lives way up in the mountains north of Hickory," she explained. "Thus far, I've been corresponding with him in conjunction with my work as an editor. Because he's a philosopher of sorts, I find him quite interesting." She turned toward Hugh and searched his face while she asked, "Would you mind if I continued to correspond with him outside the office?"

"I don't see why not," Hugh replied in his usual detached way.

"But, honey, he's a man, and a rather good-looking one at that. Wouldn't it make you uncomfortable if we wrote?"

Hugh's blond eyebrows knitted together as he thought. "Well, I think it's important that you have friends who understand your love for music and literature and stuff. I suppose this guy is really into those kinds of things, isn't he?"

"As a matter of fact, he is." Audra masked her surprise at such insight from Hugh. Was this the same man who showed passion only for soulless numbers on computer screens? She suspected her husband was, indeed, a many-layered man.

"And, Audra," he went on, "I just can't get excited over your long-haired music or the books you like or the scenery you rave about." Hugh's eyes flicked to the rearview mirror, then back again to the road ahead. "I've honestly tried, but I just don't look at the world like you do. So I think it's important for you to have friends who understand your point of view."

Audra found herself speechless. Then with a nervous giggle, she said, "Hugh, I think that's very considerate. I had no idea you understood our differences so well. And if you truly think it wouldn't be inappropriate for me to write this man, then I'll continue the friendship."

"Well, I don't see why you were troubled by it in the first place," he mumbled, "but then I don't understand a lot of things about you."

CHAPTER 15

Audra was still grinning when she exclaimed, "Nor I, you!"

The letters continued, this time to and from her mailbox at the Nashville apartment. Sometimes Craig poked fun at wild creatures:

> Just like my grandpappy and grandmammy used to do, the birds are sassin' at one another these splendid mornings. What could they be bickerin' about anyway? The world's too fine.

And at other times he wrote in awe:

> When tiny blossoms of wild strawberry and May-apple and chickweed first peek out of a tangled forest floor, I know only God could plan for beauty in these meanest of places.

Each time Audra read his words, she felt strangely warmed and wondered what it was that drew her to this man. Envy of his carefree lifestyle? The enchanting scenery he described? His perpetual optimism? His caring, perhaps? Whatever the reasons, she was growing more confident about her ability to keep the friendship in proper perspective.

At the same time, she was attempting to accept Hugh for who he was. Because any hope that her husband would change had shriveled and almost disappeared, Audra determined to gather her nurturing from wherever she could find it: from her daily relationship with God, her women's Bible study, her church family, her children's weekly phone calls, the occasional letters from Julie, and, yes, from Craig McGregor's moving prose.

Chapter 16

After Andy's graduation from college, one busy month blended into another until summer peaked with a few ninety-degree days near July's end. That was when Audra, representing her publishing company, boarded a plane and flew off to the cooler climes of the Pacific Northwest.

Tacoma's evening rush-hour traffic had long since passed by the time she retrieved her luggage and rented a car. Welcoming the large-lettered signs along Interstate 5, she breathed, "Good! I won't have any trouble finding my exit." The coordinator for the writer's conference had informed Audra that the motel where the university had reserved her a room was visible from the freeway.

"Sure enough!" she sang out, spying the inn's well-lighted façade rising several stories into the twilight sky.

Moments later she glanced up at the turtle-green underbody of a military plane as it swooped low over the parking lot. Gathering her suitcases, Audra trudged toward the red-canopied entrance. Although her watch said nine-thirty, fatigue reminded her that it was nearly midnight in Nashville—and even later in her hometown.

Entering the deserted lobby, she noted a glassed-in corridor decorated with tall tropical plants, obviously a sheltered walkway to the motel's restaurant.

"Well, I won't starve this week," she thought, struggling with her luggage toward the registration desk.

A young woman flashed her a smile only briefly before tending to the business of forms and Audra's key. "You have a

CHAPTER 16

no-smoking room on the second floor," she said in a crisp voice. "And here's a packet of materials from the university. They've asked me to tell you that a map to the campus and your cafeteria meal tickets are enclosed and that they'd like you present for the opening assembly at 9:00 a.m."

"Thank you!" Audra replied, heading for the elevator.

"Oh, I almost forgot," the receptionist called after her. "I hope it was all right to rent the room next to yours to a Mr. McGregor. He said he was a business colleague."

Audra's shock nearly caused her to stumble over a suitcase. "Craig McGregor?" she asked, hoping the blithe tone properly masked her surprise.

"Yes," the woman said.

Panic swept over Audra while she doubled the effort to disguise her emotions. "That's fine," she said. "Mr. McGregor is one of our authors."

Escaping into the elevator, she pushed a button and waited for the doors to close. Her mind raced frantically. *How could Craig be here in Washington State? And how could he ask for a room next to mine? What will these people think, anyway?*

Moments later she emerged from the elevator and quickly found her room. Glancing at the doors on either side of hers, she wondered which belonged to Craig. Her fingers trembled as she slipped the key into the lock and scurried inside. Then Audra stopped dead in her tracks when she spotted the door to an adjoining room. *With my luck, Craig's on the other side.*

Tiptoeing around, she determined to be extra quiet and decided to forego showering that night. Before climbing into bed, however, Audra considered returning to the front desk and asking the receptionist for a different room. But then the manager might inquire if there was something wrong with her accommodations. And how would she answer? She certainly couldn't say, "The room's fine. It's just that the fellow in the adjoining apartment is too sensitive, too caring." No, changing rooms would only draw more attention to the situation.

Audra clicked her tongue in disgust. She thought she had filed Craig McGregor neatly under "platonic friends" and had left him there. But now she recognized the stirrings within her

THE TEMPTING OF AUDRA GREY

as something other than platonic. They were an odd mix, part alarm, part pleasure. She had to admit that the mere knowledge that Craig was so close excited her. Too tired to get her Bible from her suitcase, Audra picked up the bedside Gideon Bible and opened it to 2 Peter 2:9: "The Lord knoweth how to deliver the godly out of temptations." "Thank You, Father," she prayed. Then she read the rest of the verse: "And to reserve the unjust unto the day of judgment to be punished."

"Yes, thank You," Audra said again. She then lay back on the pillow, letting her anxiety slowly fade into sleep.

Dressed in a lightweight teal business suit and creamy blouse, the editor picked up her briefcase. She was hoping to reach the car before Craig appeared. But as soon as she emerged from her room, he came out of his. And just as she had suspected, the mountain man was camped on the other side of that door in her wall.

At once she noticed a pleasant change about him. The summer sun had bronzed his skin, giving Craig the look of an outdoor athlete. But the laughing, pale eyes never changed. They beamed at her with flattering approval.

"Surprise, Miz Audra! I thought I'd hone my writing skills this week and revisit a beautiful part of the country. Even purchased a new suit for the occasion!" He tugged at the hem of his light-blue jacket, then offered to take her briefcase.

A sudden melting of resolve disconcerted her. "I can carry it myself, thank you!" she huffed, whisking down the hall.

When Craig caught up with her at the elevator, Audra glanced nervously about, then edged closer to him. "How could you ask for a room right next to mine?" she hissed. "Didn't you even consider what the receptionist might think of such an arrangement?"

He appeared confused, then brightened. "Oh, I made it clear that our relationship is strictly a business one."

"I'm sure most people do when they—they—" The gaping elevator rescued her. After the couple stepped inside, Audra smoldered silently a few moments before continuing, "In my capacity as an editor of a Christian publishing house, my reputation must remain impeccable." Her voice took on a pleading note. "I've tried to explain this to you before, but you just don't seem to understand. I'm kind of like a minister,

CHAPTER 16

Craig. I have to guard against anything that might damage my witness."

After the elevator bell halted her speech, Audra hurried through the lobby. But Craig kept up with her, panting, "But, Miz Audra, I think you're overreacting. I'd never do anything to mar your reputation. And I'm sure that sweet lady didn't entertain one surly thought about us." Then, as they stepped outside, in contrast to the dazzling day, Craig's face clouded. "You're really angry with me, aren't you?"

"I don't get angry," she informed him. "It's indignation I feel."

With a slow, playful grin, he queried, "The righteous kind, I hope?"

"Of course!" she replied. Suddenly seized with an unbearable urge to laugh, Audra turned on her heels and fled to the car.

His parting words trailed after her, "Remember, the Bible says you're not supposed to let the sun go down on your wrath!"

Then I've got the entire day to seethe, Mr. McGregor!

Audra guided the rented Chevy through quiet residential streets to a stoplight, where traffic noticeably thickened. Then she followed a busy avenue through a sprawl of fast-food restaurants, gas stations, and other businesses just waking up.

Turning off the main thoroughfare, she soon spied the steeple of the university's church, then the school's tall, shaded buildings across the street. The scene—a mix of stone and brick, of old and new architectural styles, of ivy trailing here and there—inspired an intense attack of nostalgia. Audra sighed, trying to refocus her attention on the job at hand. Today she would play the role as teacher and mentor; she wanted to talk in sparkling sentences that would inspire writers to produce literature that breathed on its own. She would mingle with her students and encourage the hesitant ones. With these goals weighing on her mind, she practically marched up the street.

All morning Craig McGregor seemed to avoid her, but she was quite aware of his presence—in the cafeteria, at the registration table, among the audience echoing with excited voices. Wherever she went, his impressive form stood out. A unique presence—an aura—about Craig made it impossible for him to blend into a crowd.

THE TEMPTING OF AUDRA GREY

Then, unexpectedly, the mountain man showed up in her afternoon class entitled "Words That Count."

She acknowledged him with a polite nod, then addressed the class in a teacherly voice, "During this hour we're going to discuss the two most important parts of a sentence—the noun and the verb." Distributing handouts, she continued, explaining the writer's need to detect weak verbs, such as *is* or *was*, and substitute stronger, specific verbs in their places.

Up shot Craig's hand. "Uh, ma'am, where I come from, people use *was* a lot. It's a part of our vernacular. If I were to prune all those *wases* out, the dialogue would lose its country flavor."

With his challenge, Audra's mind clicked into gear, taking control lest she crumble before him and the other dozen-or-so students. "I'm glad you mentioned that at this time," she said primly. "It's true that, for the most part, people talk in a loose, comfortable style, which does include weak verbs." She smiled sweetly at Craig. "Therefore, leave your *wases* in the dialogue where you think they're appropriate. But"—she raised a finger in warning—"in the tags, the narrative, the descriptive portions, utilize powerful verbs that pack a wallop."

Although Craig fell silent for the rest of the class, Audra noticed that he was studying her intently. She soon discovered why when she passed his desk and looked down at a picture he had sketched—of her! In the lifelike sketch, she stood with hands tucked into her skirt pockets, the blazer gapped in front and the blouse underneath draped loosely. Craig had drawn her face tilted upward in a haughty gesture. For a brief moment her glance grazed his; then she went on with the lecture.

Later that afternoon, Audra slipped unnoticed from the campus. She was finished for the day, and weariness, like leaden weights, dragged at her body.

Making it all the way back to the inn without encountering Craig McGregor again, Audra quickly slipped into her room and collapsed on the bed. Sleep overtook her in minutes.

When she awoke hours later, feeling dazed, the sun had already rounded the roofs and was sinking lazily toward the horizon. Slowly and stiffly, she rose to her feet and switched on the light. At the sight of her wrinkled suit, she groaned. "Why

CHAPTER 16

didn't I take it off!"

After changing into a bathrobe, Audra's toe caught on something white. She bent down and picked up a large index card, which had obviously been slipped from the next room under the door. There was the familiar artist's hand:

> The sun'll be setting soon. Have you forgiven me yet, or do I have to do some sort of penance first? I'm so sorry, Miz Audra. I'd never intentionally hurt you—or your reputation.

She hunted for a pen and scrawled back:

> No penance necessary, sir. Salvation is free, remember? And, yes, you're forgiven.

"It's just natural to slip a little Bible instruction in there," she thought smugly as she stuffed the card back under the door.

On her return from a refreshing shower, she noticed that another index card had appeared.

> Thank you, kind lady! Would you let me make up for my blundering by treating you to supper at the restaurant downstairs?

She quickly wrote back:

> No, thank you! I'm exhausted. Am going to sleep. Good night, Mr. McGregor!

While Audra lay in bed, paging through her Bible and reading a commentary on Job, she heard a swishing sound. She could see the telltale white again at the foot of the door, but ignored it and read on.

When she studied the tenth verse of the first chapter, Satan's challenge to God about upright Job, Audra paraphrased it to apply to her own situation: "Hast not thou made a hedge about Audra Grey, and about her house, and about all that she has?

THE TEMPTING OF AUDRA GREY

Thou hast blessed the work of her hands. . . . Take away that hedge, though, and she will curse thee."

"Would I?" she pondered. "I seriously doubt it."

Then she read on in chapter 2, where Satan brings another challenge before the Lord: "But put forth thine hand now, and touch his bone and his flesh, and he will curse thee to thy face."

"Hmmm!" Could something like that be taking place in her own life? She had already suspected that Satan was behind her husband's aloofness. And, as she had wondered before, did Satan himself send Craig McGregor along—and now place that big, handsome hunk of humanity in the adjoining motel room? Did the cunning Beelzebub inspire Craig to write sweet notes and slip them under her door? She could well imagine the devil sneering, "Give me just a few nights of this side-by-side situation. Mrs. Grey is so starved for affection by now that she'll soon fling open that door and throw herself into McGregor's arms."

Audra shook off her imaginings, then slid off the bed and bent low to read:

> Sweet dreams, beautiful lady! And remember, my door to your room is wide open. If someone should break in during the night, simply call out, and I'll knock down your door and trounce the scoundrel.

She couldn't help but smile at the chivalrous phrases. Break down her door, indeed! Hugh would never— "Hugh!" She gasped. She was supposed to have phoned him that morning but was so upset about Craig's surprise appearance that the call had slipped her mind.

It was already eleven o'clock in the East. Quickly, she dialed long distance, recalling the digits of her credit card.

"Hello, darling!" she exclaimed as soon as she heard her husband's voice. "I'm sorry I didn't call earlier."

"That's all right," he said. "I didn't even think about it."

"Oh!" she replied, a little deflated. "And how are things going there?"

"The usual hassle. End-of-the month reports, you know."

She chuckled. "Isn't it something how the end of the month

CHAPTER 16

keeps coming around so fast?" She filled a sudden silence with, "Tell me, Hugh, don't you want to hear what I'm doing?"

"I suppose."

She wondered how her husband would react if she said, "Well, actually my handsome bodyguard in the next room just asked me to dinner, but I'm too tired. His door is open, though, in case I need him during the night."

Hugh would probably comment in his usual monotone, "That's nice."

Audra reported on her day's activities. "And my schedule for tomorrow is already filled with the names of prospective authors."

"What for?"

"That's when I give each writer about ten minutes to tell me about a book they want to write or are writing. It's a great way to discover future authors for the publishing house."

"Sounds boring to me."

"It'll be tiring sitting in one place most of the day. But I look forward to meeting lots of new people, and it's actually fun."

"If you say so," Hugh replied.

Audra smiled. "I feel sorry for most of them, though. They get pretty nervous. I guess we editors are intimidating creatures. I do my best to put them at ease."

She could tell by Hugh's silence that he was eager to get to sleep. She felt like screaming into the receiver, "Listen here, Hugh Grey! I need you to whisper something passionate into my ear. Tell me you can't stand my being gone another three nights!" Instead she asked, "Do you miss me?"

"You're usually away at this time anyway."

She sighed. Her husband was in no mood for talk of any kind. She felt deserted, and a sudden wash of loneliness chilled her. "Good night, Hugh!"

"Good night!"

Audra dropped to her knees beside the bed and began, "Dear Father . . ." But other thoughts kept intruding on her nightly prayers. She felt torn, and like Job, caught between two titanic forces. Perhaps her imaginings hadn't strayed too far from reality after all, because the same question returned again and again, "Can I make it clear to Thursday night without opening that door?"

Chapter 17

All day they approached her. The timid ones, the bold ones, the humble, the vain—they came with their offerings of manuscripts. And after hours of sitting in a rigid-backed chair, the editor grew painfully stiff.

For the most part, the writers were amateurs. But the teacher in Audra relished showing them how to improve their writing. At the same time, she took extra care not to wound, wondering whether everyone was as sensitive as these fledgling writers. Or was it their creative natures that made them more vulnerable to criticism?

At her last appointment for the afternoon, a plump poet, accompanied by a one-man cheering section—her husband— eased through the door.

With much of Mrs. Tuttle bulging over either side of her chair, the interview began. Right away Audra liked the woman, her enthusiasm, and her lively eyes that laughed back at the world through thick glasses. Mrs. Tuttle was, indeed, a creative soul, but one whose appearance definitely lacked refinement. An out-of-style dress stretched across her out-of-shape body, while her brown-and-white hair hung limp and stringy. And no makeup offered color to the pale, round face.

Becoming more fascinated with the couple than with the manuscript she held, Audra studied this married paradox before her. In contrast to his overweight wife, Mr. Tuttle had kept himself lean. He was fairly handsome, with thick black hair, graying somewhat around the ears. Well groomed, he wore a suit

CHAPTER 17

and tie that would have fitted nicely into any business community. Yet the distinguished-looking man genuinely adored the homely woman at his side.

While Mrs. Tuttle described the theme of her poetry, her husband nodded, then squeezed her hand. His gaze brimmed with admiration.

Skimming over a few poems, Audra quickly became aware of an ache deep inside—an ache she thought had left her months before. Now it returned and lay like a stone in the pit of her stomach. And with the ache came the memory of Hugh's hollow-sounding voice over the phone—so different from the touch, the tenderness, the bond apparent between these unique people.

Audra commented, "You definitely have talent, Mrs. Tuttle."

Before she could continue, the husband interjected, "She's a talented girl all right! She sees God's hand in every little detail—"

"Yes, I can tell by your writing that you've been blessed with special insight," the editor said. "I'm sorry to tell you, however, that my company rarely publishes poetry. Nowadays only big-name poets usually make it into book print."

Audra watched the man stroke his wife's hand in a consoling gesture while he declared, "Those authors weren't always big names, you know. They had to start out at one time just like Sarah here."

"You're right," Audra beamed at him. "And I think a good start would be for her to submit the poems individually to various inspirational magazines. There are several represented here at the conference. Have you made appointments with any of them?" she asked the woman.

Mrs. Tuttle chuckled demurely. "My husband signed me up on just about every list. He thinks I'm the next Pulitzer Prize winner."

Audra's smile faded, and what she uttered next sounded like a proclamation. "You're a very lucky woman, Mrs. Tuttle, to have such support. Few writers get that kind of encouragement from anyone." She rose to shake their hands. "I'm so glad I got the chance to meet you today. Thank you for coming!"

The couple disappeared while Audra looked after them. She felt as if she had just viewed some rare treasure in a museum.

THE TEMPTING OF AUDRA GREY

"Perhaps that's what intimacy looks like—in person," she thought. And although she realized that coveting was sin, Audra still found herself longing for only a small portion of the kind of intimacy the odd poet shared with her husband.

As she cleared her section of the desk and reloaded her briefcase, a hand brushed Audra's shoulder.

She nearly gasped when she heard the drawl that caught so poignantly at her emotions. "Ma'am, your sign-up sheet was all filled before I could scratch my name on it, and I have an idea for a new book."

Not now! I don't have the energy to keep my feelings from showing.

"May I steal just a few minutes to run a synopsis by you?" Craig asked. "I need your advice as to whether the story is even worth writing."

Audra stood face to face with him then, gathering what strength she could muster. "I would love to hear your synopsis, Craig, but at the moment, every joint in my body is fast turning to cement. If I don't go to the car, put on my sneakers, and walk for a good hour, I'll surely turn into a statue."

"Statue!" He breathed the word like a prayer. "Yes! I'd love to sculpt you. Let's see—not in wood, not in clay, but in marble, rich creamy marble from—"

"Please, Craig!" Audra's voice broke. "Don't say such things—not now!" She was begging, and she despised herself for losing her professional façade. But her mind spun with a picture of the homely Mrs. Tuttle and Hugh's deadpan replies. Her own husband hadn't even missed her, and here was this man—practically a stranger—wanting to cast her image in stone!

Audra clenched her teeth, willing away anything else that might clog her mind even more. *I'm a statue all right! A statue of brittle glass, which might splinter into a thousand pieces at any moment.*

Craig's voice dropped to a whisper. "Are those tears? Oh, I've blundered again." He looked crestfallen. "I guess I've been dwelling up in the hills so long I can't even come down into civilization anymore without charging around like some ignorant bull in a shop full of Ming vases."

CHAPTER 17

In spite of herself, Audra smiled at the rearranged cliché. "It's not you, my friend. It's— it's—a personal problem I was just reminded of," she stammered. Excusing herself, she whirled around and scurried out the door.

It seemed lately she was forever running from Craig McGregor, and he was forever catching up with her. "OK, but if I'm truly your friend, you would tell me your trouble," he insisted, "so I could nod and sympathize as all good mountain folk do. Can you share it with me?" he asked.

Not with a friend like you, a friend who spouts phrases that could charm the skin off a copperhead. She winced. *Another McGregorism! He's infiltrating my brain.* Then she declared aloud, "Maybe sometime, but not now."

Late-afternoon sunbeams trickled around a canopy of cedar branches that shadowed the cobbled path to the parking lot. When they arrived at her car, Craig lingered, watching Audra gather the socks and walking shoes.

Suddenly he surprised her by offering, "Here! Let me put those on you!"

Before she knew what was happening, she sat half out of the vehicle while the mountain man knelt in his new suit on the asphalt below. Then with great care he removed her high heels.

Astonished, she protested, "Mr. McGregor! Don't you think this is highly improper? What will people say?" Her heart was thumping crazily as his big hands caressed her feet and gently slipped on each sock.

"No one will notice over here in this corner," he said, then observed, "You even have beautiful feet, Miz Audra. Yes, you'd make an exquisite sculpture," Craig repeated softly.

She could feel something warm and titillating prickle the nerves in her feet, then rise and spread until all her senses tingled. She reacted instantly by jerking her foot out of his grasp, then feverishly tying the remaining shoe herself. *The thoughts are roosting.* Then the words slipped out, "But they mustn't build nests."

Still on his knees, Craig looked up quizzically. "Did I miss something?"

"Yes, something important," she said, her tone edged with

113

impatience. "I was trying to tell you in a kind way that a man who is not a woman's husband does not put shoes on her. It just isn't—isn't kosher."

"What if we pretended you were my kid sister?"

These are not sisterly feelings. "There are times when pretending isn't appropriate, Craig, and this is one of them. I wouldn't want my witness to the people on this campus tainted in any way."

"I understand," he said, deliberately looking around before he helped her up. "But I really doubt that anyone saw. And Miz Audra, if you don't mind my telling you so, you're just too inhibited. You're so afraid of anything that might even resemble impropriety that you've locked yourself into a cubbyhole. You need to relax and enjoy life and the caring people around you—people like me."

Audra felt defensive. "My space isn't that small, Craig. It includes a lot of beautiful people, but I'm afraid I'll never be able to relax completely around you."

A strange mix of hurt and bewilderment passed over Craig's face before he asked, "What's wrong with me?"

"You're too—too—wonderful," she replied flatly. There! It was out. Now he knew.

A sudden insight came into the pale eyes. "Tell me truthfully, Miz Audra, has your husband ever put your shoes and socks on your feet? Has he ever kissed each of your bare toes first? Has he—"

"Stop!" she blurted. "That really isn't any of your business."

"If I'm your friend, it is."

"You can't be my friend, Craig, not in the true sense of the word."

His face searched hers. "Because you're attracted to me?"

"I didn't say that." Then Audra's voice quivered as she turned away from him. "Would you please leave me to myself?" she asked quietly. "I really need to be alone awhile. Maybe we can talk later."

She heard the soft footsteps trudging off through the trees.

Chapter 18

When at last Audra straggled back to the motel room, her gaze fell immediately upon another white card on the carpet.

> I feel perplexed and clumsy, like a fish flopping around on sand. Please talk to me, Miz Audra! How come I keep upsetting you so?

She dropped the note in a wastebasket, then sank wearily onto the edge of the bed. Her tiredness wasn't all physical, she realized. It stemmed from taut nerves. First she had dealt with an endless stream of hopeful writers, and, however gingerly, she still had trodden upon some tender hearts that day. Now there was the tender heart of Craig McGregor to deal with—plus a barrage of her own warring emotions, which seemed, of late, to accompany the mere mention of his name.

Audra sat, quiet and contemplative, feeling the stale air close around her. "I'm not being fair," she brooded. "I owe him some kind of explanation."

Changing into a comfortable pair of slacks and a silky blouse, she lay down on her stomach in front of the adjoining-room door and called softly through it, "Craig, are you there?"

In seconds she heard his deep voice, "Yes. How are you feeling now?"

"A little better." She hesitated. "I guess I should explain some things. Do you have time to listen?"

"I've got all night, ma'am."

THE TEMPTING OF AUDRA GREY

She drew in a deep breath, then began. "You called me inhibited earlier, and I suppose I am, if that means taking my faith seriously. Even stray thoughts aren't allowed."

She heard Craig's low whistle. "You're not trapped in a cubbyhole, Miz Audra, but in stocks!"

"Maybe you perceive it that way, Craig, but I've managed just fine all these years. It's not difficult to serve Someone as caring as the Lord, and there's a certain freedom in our relationship."

"Perhaps . . ."

"Anyway," she went on, "ever since my children left for college and I've had to live so far from home, I've grown more and more miserable."

"I'm sorry." The tone on the other side of the door was truly sympathetic. Then his concern took a new twist. "Tell me, what's your husband like?"

"Oh, he's quite handsome, a staunch worker in the church, and a good provider for our family."

"But what's he really like, Miz Audra? Does he love you?"

"I think he does."

"You don't know for sure?" Craig sounded puzzled.

"Well, it's kind of hard to tell," she said. "Hugh isn't the demonstrative type."

"You mean he doesn't lavish you with kisses as soon as you return home and tell you how beautiful you are and things like that?"

"Not exactly," she admitted with a giggle. "He's pretty reserved."

"I see."

"Anyway, as a result of this forced separation from my family, I think I might be suffering from a bit of depression. It's not bad. It comes and goes. But when I add spiritual dilemmas to it—like trying to put my friendship with you in its proper place—the depression sort of engulfs me. At times I feel as if I might drown in it."

There was a long silence before Craig replied, "I'm beginning to understand. You must feel horrible. And I didn't help matters any, did I, by insisting on dressing your pretty little feet this evening?"

CHAPTER 18

"No, Craig, you didn't."

There was another awkward pause, then, "Miz Audra, a woman likes to feel desirable. Does Hugh make you feel desirable?"

"That isn't important." She evaded his question. "What's important is, can you and I be friends—platonic friends? Or are we going to have to stop seeing and writing each other altogether?"

Craig cleared his throat. "Then I would become the depressed one. Let me suggest something. I'm very strong-willed and, believe me, I'd never cross that imaginary line of propriety, Miz Audra. Why don't you observe for yourself what a gentleman and platonic friend I can be by joining me tomorrow for a sightseeing tour? We could drive up to view Mount Rainier first, then take a trip across the peninsula and on over to the coast."

A thrill shot through Audra at the thought of such a tour. "That sounds wonderfully refreshing," she said. "But, to be honest, I'm not sure if I can handle my—my— feelings right now."

She could well imagine the sparkle in Craig's eyes when he entreated, "If I promise not to tell you even once how stunning you look and I vow to keep my hands off your feet—in fact, I won't touch you at all—will you come with me then?"

"Well," she considered aloud, "I had already planned to venture up into the hills myself as soon as tomorrow morning's assembly ended." She pursed her lips in thought. "And I don't have any responsibilities at the university again until the panel discussion on Thursday afternoon."

"I know the territory better than you," he coaxed.

"All right," she said finally, "as long as we can meet back here at the inn. Everyone who knows me should be at the conference then."

"Still worried about your reputation?" he teased.

"Of course!"

With that matter settled, they continued to talk. Although the shut door stood between them like a wooden sentinel, nothing blocked the carefree communication that flowed back and forth.

Audra turned over and, folding her arms under her head, listened intently while Craig told her about his short time in an orphanage. She knew by his enthusiasm that he enjoyed the telling. Audra noticed, too, that traffic noises were beginning to dwindle outside the walls.

THE TEMPTING OF AUDRA GREY

When a lull came in the conversation, she wondered aloud, "I don't understand how a boy pushed from an orphanage to one foster home after another could turn out so well-rounded."

"That's easy to answer," he said. "Most of those homes were provided by relatives, some close, some shirttail. But every one of them taught me something different—how to draw, how to whittle and sculpt, how to farm and live off the land and streams around us. They passed on to me our rich Anglo-Saxon heritage. Also, I was born with a powerful curiosity, an insatiable desire to learn, learn, learn." His voice trailed off.

Audra then shared with Craig incidents from her growing-up years. They talked on and on, unencumbered by the restraints of society. Occasionally, his quick humor sent her literally rolling around on the carpet, caught in spasms of breathy laughter.

While he held her ears captive, Craig took the opportunity to sketch in words the beautiful character of a great aunt who had pioneered on the Blue Ridge. "Her life might make an inspiring plot for my next book," Craig said. "What do you think?"

The editor in Audra perked up. "If you tell the story in the same charming style as in *Eddie Mae and Me*, I'd say you'd write another winner."

She heard his chuckle. "*Eddie Mae and Me* isn't a winner yet, Miz Audra."

"It will be," she assured him. Glancing over at her travel alarm, she gasped. "It's way after midnight!"

"Well, if you'll recall, I told you I had all night."

"Do you know what this reminds me of?" She giggled.

"What?"

"Of when I was four years old. I used to keep an imaginary friend behind the kitchen door, and any time life got especially hard, I'd slip behind that door and talk to my friend. Her name was Jackie. I could tell her anything, because she always understood."

"That's what friends are for, you know—understanding."

"Yes, well, my mother became a little nervous about my relying on this imaginary friend. Eventually she took me to our family doctor. He told her, though, not to worry, that as soon as

CHAPTER 18

I got into school and acquired real friends, imaginary Jackie would disappear."

"Did she?" Craig asked.

"Until now," she said. "Good night, Jackie!"

He tittered, forcing his voice to a higher pitch. "Good night, Miz Audra!"

Chapter 19

Only a few gauzy clouds skirted an otherwise perfect summer sky when Audra left the university and drove back to her motel.

Excited about the adventure that lay ahead, she quickly changed into hiking clothes, grabbed a sweater, then met Craig in the lobby.

"Ready for the grand tour?" he asked, smiling his usual generous way. A light jacket was slung over his shoulder.

"I'm eager for it," she exclaimed, spotting a white paper sack in his grip. "What's in the bag?"

"You'll find out," he said secretively, then led her to his car.

A little distance south, Craig turned off the freeway and headed east until the urban scenery changed into country suburbs. A few small shopping centers still cropped up to remind them that civilization lurked nearby.

"You know," Audra declared, "if someone kidnapped me and set me down right here, I'd think I was still in Tennessee."

Craig grinned. "There are similarities," he agreed. "But just be patient. Soon you'll notice some mighty big differences!"

The dense green of Scotch broom bordered the roadway as the car ventured through a more wooded area and farmlands beyond. When a logging truck rumbled past, Audra couldn't help but gawk at the load it carried.

"If you think those logs are big, you should see some of the giants in Mount Rainier National Park," Craig said.

"But I thought we were going there."

"Just to the edge," he told her, "past the Carbon River, where

CHAPTER 19

we can get a good view of the old fellow."

To her deflated "oh," he explained, "You see, there isn't enough time to get any closer to the mountain and still be able to catch a ferry to Vashon Island, then wander on to the coast before sunset. The days are long here, but not that long!" Then he glanced over at her and, in a softer tone, offered, "If you'd rather spend more time on the mountain, Miz Audra, we could forget the coast."

"No, thank you!" she exclaimed. "I must see the ocean. Anyway, there's something about a seashore that helps clear cobwebs from the mind."

He grinned knowingly. "There is, indeed!"

Climbing into higher country, they came upon a small town with storefronts that looked transplanted from an Old West movie set. In the midst of the rustic setting, something bulbous and blue jetted up.

"What's that?" Audra asked.

"Let's go see!" Craig swerved onto a side street and halted before a quaint white church with an odd bell tower and steeple.

"It looks Turkish or Russian, doesn't it?" Audra said.

"Yep! Now my curiosity's up. I'd love to while away the day here and talk to folks, discover how this town evolved." Craig beamed. "But then we'd never make it to the coast. We'd better be going!"

A smile lingered on Audra's lips as they found their way back to the main road. She noticed how totally relaxed she had become in the mountain man's company. It was as if they viewed the world through the same eyes. Who else would veer off course on the spur of the moment to investigate a strange-looking steeple? Here so far from home, far from time clocks and committee meetings, Audra felt free to share in some of Craig McGregor's vagabond spirit—"just for a day!" she reminded herself.

When the blacktop deteriorated to gravel and potholes, though, Audra's carefree attitude began to desert her. "Uh, are you sure you know where you're going?" she asked in a timid voice.

"Trust me!" came the reply.

She leaned back and watched the trees arch thick over the roadway. Ferns and other undergrowth crept off in every direction, giving the day an illusion of coolness.

121

THE TEMPTING OF AUDRA GREY

Then quite abruptly, the trees parted, and a colossal snow-crowned peak with jagged patches of purple poking through loomed before them.

Audra gasped. "Oh! It's more beautiful than I ever imagined. Snow in July—unbelievable!"

Craig looked pleased at her reaction, then pulled over to the side of the road. There on a grassy knoll, beneath the impressive visage of Mount Rainier, they picnicked on the contents of the mysterious white bag.

Except for one passing car, an immense quiet hung over the wilderness, over the fir-laden slopes that dipped low, then climbed to the broad shoulders of the mountain.

After a long spell of silence between the couple, Audra finally said, "You were awfully considerate to buy us sandwiches and fruit for lunch."

"Don't mention it, ma'am! It's all part of the tour package," he teased. Then Craig clicked a few snapshots of Audra in front of the mountain.

"So much beauty—" he began, then caught himself. "Are you ready to head west? Next stop is Point Defiance back in Tacoma."

"Is that where we catch the ferry?"

"Uh-huh."

Pausing for one last look at the mountain, Audra speculated, "I imagine that old guy can become pretty cantankerous at times. He's just putting on his good face for us today."

She could sense that Craig wanted to comment but was keeping his thoughts to himself. "He's doing his utmost to prove himself platonic," she mused.

A Steller's jay called a raucous goodbye before it dove in search of any leftover crumbs.

The hours seemed to stand still that afternoon. First there was the ferry ride from Point Defiance to Tahlequah on the southernmost tip of Vashon Island. Then, wandering the winding island roads, they drove to the northernmost tip of the island.

"See how the trees droop and look tattered!" she pointed out. "Kind of reminds me of Louisiana swamplands."

"Well, they do get lots of rain here," Craig commented.

CHAPTER 19

"I wish we had time to explore. There's something adventuresome about an island, don't you think?"

"Yep!" he replied. "Makes me feel like Huckleberry Finn."

"Then I'll be Tom Sawyer," she quipped.

Later, on another ferry, sailing this time toward Southworth, Audra stood on deck and watched gulls swoop and soar above the water. The breeze tousled her hair, but she paid no heed. Here was tranquility: The full sun warming her, the wake spreading out from the boat, cottages peeking from wooded hills encircling Puget Sound, the hum of the motors under her feet. "I could stay on board forever and never tire of it," she said.

Craig nodded. "I could too."

Soon they walked unsteadily across the rocking deck, hurrying back to their car before the boat shuddered and thumped to a stop.

As they continued their journey, dropping south toward the highway that would take them farther west, the sun was beginning its downward trek toward the horizon. "Do you think we'll make it to the coast in time to see it?" Audra worried.

"In plenty of time for a nice long stroll on the seashore," he assured her. "This time of year the sun doesn't set until around nine o'clock; then twilight lingers a long while."

Audra spotted gray clouds in the distance. "Unless a storm ruins things."

"But the storms here are mostly gentle," he informed her, "nothing like the noisemakers we Southerners are used to."

When they neared the ocean, Audra's excitement grew. "I can feel it! There's new freshness in the air."

Coming to an intersection, Craig turned left toward Ocean Shores. Trees and dunes hid the view until they turned right and drove directly out onto the sand.

"Craig!" Audra cried out. "What are you doing?"

"In Washington State, cars are allowed to drive on the beaches."

"Are you sure we won't get stuck?"

"No." Then he pulled to a stop. "Now, quit your fretting, ma'am, and take a look!"

Audra's breath caught in her throat when her gaze swept the vast blue of water, the waves crashing ashore. "Let's walk!" she shouted against the sound of the surf.

123

THE TEMPTING OF AUDRA GREY

After Craig helped her put on her sweater, he donned his jacket. Then they strolled up the beach. Audra could barely make out the forms of some far-off hills melding into the clouds.

After a while Craig asked, "Well, how did I do today—as a platonic friend, I mean?"

"If I were grading you, I'd give you an 'A'," she said.

He looked relieved, and they continued their stroll.

When the sun began to turn the clouds to a kaleidoscope of color, the twosome dropped to the sand, sitting silently in wonder.

With her knees drawn up to her chin, Audra could feel her eyes tearing. "Thank you, Craig, for giving me this day! What we've seen—especially this sunset—is beyond value."

"You're most welcome, Miz Audra. Now, tell me, can't you just feel the Creator in that fuchsia sky?"

She giggled. "No, Craig! I see the created." Then she asked, "Do you think God arranged this just for us?"

"He might have."

All day they had carefully sidestepped any talk about personal things, Audra reflected, and yet she was sure Craig also felt the strong current between them. It was as real as the waves and dying colors they were watching.

While ambling back to the car, he asked, "Are you hungry?"

"Famished!"

"Then let's get something to eat at that motel over there." He pointed across the dunes.

Audra hesitated. "Only if we go Dutch."

He looked disgruntled, but conceded, "All right!"

Minutes later the couple was settled at a corner table in a glassed-in lounge overlooking the dunes and sea. Soft music, soft lights, and soft voices surrounded them. Adding to the cozy warmth of brown hues, rough-cut boards paneled the walls away from the view.

Still avoiding personal talk, they discussed the replanted clearcuts they had seen on their way there. That led Craig to the subject of his small orchard.

"I water those apple trees, prune them, spread fertilizer at their feet. And when their branches grow heavy with fruit, I prop them up. Even in winter, when a farmer should rest, I'm

CHAPTER 19

out there dusting snow off their bare arms." He smiled. "I guess those trees are the closest things to children I've ever had."

Audra digested what he had said before replying, "I think God is like that in caring for us. He never rests either. And He's just as gentle, not allowing too much to bear on us at one time. He kind of nudges us along." And then her thoughts strayed to the word picture she had created for Hugh once. Ironically, Craig was the kind of "gardener" Hugh refused to become.

Abruptly, a loud statement from the next table intruded: "One time she even made asparagus jello!"

To keep from laughing outright, Audra nearly choked on a crescent roll. Craig seemed quite amused with the whole scene. As the meal progressed, talk turned to Craig's beloved mountains and the history made in the backcountry.

"Now Andrew Jackson was an interesting character," Craig said.

"You mean the President?"

"Old Hickory himself!" Craig stared out at the sea, where the few lights of trawlers dotted the darkness. "Jackson inherited a special folk culture from the borders of North Britain. You stir that culture around in the backcountry awhile, and you've got a unique kind of frontiersman."

Craig went on to relay a tale he had heard once about how Andrew Jackson had won his wife. "In plain language, he stole her from her husband."

"How barbarian!"

"Not really," Craig argued. "Jackson came from good stock. And Rachel Donelson Robards came from an eminent family. But she married badly and was dreadfully unhappy with her husband, Lewis. Although bridal abductions were the norm among rival clans, in this instance the bride went willingly."

"Didn't Lewis fight for her?"

Craig emitted a wry chuckle. "Well, there was a bit of a fuss. But once Andrew threatened to cut off the other fellow's ears, old Lewis fled to higher country and was never seen since."

Audra frowned. "It's still barbarian."

"Don't you think God bends the rules some to allow for a person's culture?"

THE TEMPTING OF AUDRA GREY

"In neutral matters, perhaps, but not in moral matters," she insisted. "Sin by any other name is still sin."

"Hmmm! I think someday, Miz Audra, you're going to be mighty surprised whom you meet in heaven."

She grinned. "Perhaps. And mind you, I'm not President and Mrs. Jackson's judge. But if I'm personally going to err, Craig, I'd rather do it on the side of right than the other way around."

On their drive back to Tacoma, a light rain began to fall, and its blur against the glass was the last scene Audra remembered before dozing off.

When they reached the inn, she awoke, feeling surprisingly refreshed. Thanking him, she grasped the door handle.

"Audra!" he stopped her.

Not Miz Audra!

"I hope I don't spoil this beautiful day we've shared, but I need to ask you something." And before she could respond, Craig blurted, "Have you ever considered divorcing Hugh?"

Her reply was just as blunt. "I believe the word *divorce* shouldn't even enter a Christian's vocabulary. Vows are forever."

"Not if Hugh has broken those vows, they're not."

She came close to sneering. "Believe me! Hugh has never cheated on me."

"He may not be cheating on you, Audra, but he is cheating you out of the marriage the Lord intended for you to have." Then Craig told her, "I did quite a study on divorce once for a friend of mine who was trapped in an impossible situation. His wife withheld all love from him, physical and otherwise."

Audra cringed. The subject was brushing too close to her own "impossible situation."

Craig continued. "John, a staunch Christian like yourself, was determined to hold on at all cost. I could see how such rejection was driving him to physical and emotional ruin. So I gathered the Bible, concordances, books explaining the original Hebrew and Greek, then plunged in."

Audra listened intently.

"After all that study, I came to the conclusion that, yes, marriage is sacred and shouldn't be disregarded as easily as it was during times in Old Testament days.

CHAPTER 19

"But I also concluded that my friend had two valid grounds for divorce: First, his wife was technically an 'unbelieving spouse,' just like Paul talks about in First Corinthians, the seventh chapter. She certainly wasn't filled with Christ's love and imparting that to her husband. Just the opposite! In such cases, the apostle said if the unbelieving partner leaves, then let her do so. A brother or sister is not under bondage in such cases."

"I don't know," Audra murmured. "That's judging again—and really stretching Scripture."

"Please, hear me out!" Craig pleaded. "I found the real clincher in Matthew 19:9, where Christ Himself gives the only exception for divorce and remarriage: except it be for fornication, *porneia* in Greek. I wondered why Jesus didn't use the word for adultery there as He does further on? Could the word *porneia* encompass more than adultery? What kind of sexual sin does *porneia* include?"

Craig faced Audra squarely and asked, "Could your husband's withholding his love from you be considered *porneia* and thus, grounds for divorce?"

The question left her speechless, and she tightened her grip on the door handle again.

But Craig persisted, "Have you ever stopped to consider that God might have gotten you that job in Nashville just so you and I could meet?"

She laughed. "It's funny you should say that, because during my personal Bible studies I pretty much concluded that Satan was behind Hugh's indifference—and also behind bringing you into my life."

He shook his head slowly. "For two people so alike, we're poles apart in this instance. I wonder which one of us is right."

Audra had to admit to herself that she was wondering too. Some of what Craig had said made sense. Could she have strayed way out in a legalistic left field?

Craig's voice lowered. "Audra, if you were my wife, I would make you the most contented woman on earth. I would—"

"No, Craig!" she cut him off. "You were right. We could easily spoil this wonderful day we've shared. I'd better go in now." She paused. "Would you mind staying here a few minutes before you follow?"

THE TEMPTING OF AUDRA GREY

"I'll feel like a spy." He grinned. "But for your reputation's sake, I'll remain out here a spell." Then he added, "Remember, Audra, my half of the doorway to your room will be open all night. If you need anything, I'll be there—even if it's just a hug. Nothing more. I can be trusted, you know." Then he asked in feigned innocence, "Platonic friends do hug, don't they?"

"Only if they can do it platonically," she replied, then promptly left, dodging raindrops all the way to the entrance.

She already lay between crisp, cool sheets by the time she heard the elevator, then the sound of Craig opening the door to his room.

If you need anything, I'll be there—even if it's just a hug . . . Audra couldn't push Craig's last words out of her mind.

Julie had told her to be honest with God. So she was honest. "He's right there, Lord, on the other side of that door! He's offered to hug me. Father, do You know how long it's been since I've been genuinely hugged?" Tears trickled from her eyes. "I want to feel strong arms around me. I want—I need—to be loved, Lord."

Opening the Gideon Bible, she noticed a page in front entitled Help in the Time of Need. She ran her fingers down through the various subjects to Strength in the Time of Temptation. The texts listed on the page led her to one promise after another.

> Blessed is the man that endureth temptation: for when he is tried, he shall receive the crown of life, which the Lord hath promised to them that love him (James 1:12).

"Thank You, Lord!" she whispered. "But I need Your help to concentrate on that reward now. It seems too far away."

She turned to Hebrews 13:4-6:

> Marriage is honourable in all, and the bed undefiled: but whoremongers and adulterers God will judge.
> Let your conversation be without covetousness; and be content with such things as ye have: for he hath said, I will never leave thee, nor forsake thee.

CHAPTER 19

Forgive me, Father, for coveting Craig's attention and affection! Help me to be contented with what You've given me.

Still feeling drawn toward the door that separated her room from Craig's, Audra prayed on. She paced back and forth across the floor, repeating 1 Corinthians 10:13, which she had memorized as a child:

> There hath no temptation taken you but such as is common to man: but God is faithful, who will not suffer you to be tempted above that ye are able; but will with the temptation also make a way to escape, that ye may be able to bear it.

Climbing back into bed, Audra slept intermittently until dawn. It was then that she found another index card on the carpet.

> Goodbye, beautiful lady! I'm flying back to Charlotte this morning, but I'll see your lovely image in every cloud.
> Thanks for your sweet company yesterday.
> Your friend,
Craig

Chapter 20

Audra returned to Nashville, where rainless days were rarely hot and sultry, where the sweet scent of jasmine was fast fading from summer nights.

But the image of Craig McGregor refused to fade. Reminders of him floated everywhere: in the slow drawl of a gas-station attendant, in the spontaneous laughter of children, in a flute's song, in a stranger's bearded face. And every reminder stirred anew forbidden feelings.

Audra tried prayer. She intensified her study of the Bible. But even then the mountain man intruded.

When his letters continued, she made excuses about too much work and answered only a few. Still, they kept coming, and each time her heart leapt at the sight of his precise print. Then the message arrived that shook her very soul.

> If you should ever muster the courage to divorce Hugh, tell me truthfully, dear lady, would I have a chance with someone as beautiful as you? Would you be my wife—after a respectable waiting spell, of course?

Audra reread the words again and again that evening until the page became limp and light crept from the room. She sat unmoving in the darkness, but her mind was volleying back and forth.

Suddenly a loud ring shattered the stillness. "Audra? This is Julie. Are you all right?" Her tone was anxious. "I've felt such a

CHAPTER 20

burden to pray for you lately. What's going on?"

"Oh, Julie!" The words came rushing, and Audra couldn't stop the gloom from pouring forth. "I've been thinking of nothing but Craig McGregor. He fills my mind day and night. I don't know if it means I've fallen in love with him or what. And to make matters worse, Craig's asked me to marry him."

There was a long pause before Audra heard, "What about Hugh?"

"Craig's convinced I've got biblical grounds for divorce because my husband isn't keeping his vows to honor and cherish me, among other things."

"He may be right," Julie said. "But how do you feel about such a prospect? You've always held a narrow view of divorce."

"I still do." A sob caught at Audra's voice. "That's why I'm in such a quandary."

"Listen!" her friend coaxed, "I want you to imagine two columns, one headed 'pros' and the other one 'cons.' "

"The pros and cons of getting a divorce?" The question sounded cold and sacrilegious to Audra, coming from her own lips.

"Yes," Julie said firmly. "Now give me some positive points for taking such a drastic step."

"Well, in a worldly, legal sense, I'd be free to remarry. And I have no doubt that Craig would make a fantastic husband. He's so right-brained and interested in the same things I am. We'd really be able to communicate. And he'd never ignore me—never! I'd be free to love him without the fear of rejection. And he'd be open with his love and hug me lots and—" Audra's voice faded.

"OK," Julie said. "Now, can you think of some negative points?"

"Plenty!" Audra admitted. "First of all, my children would be devastated, and our divorce could reduce their chances for lasting marriages someday. Then there are my parents and Hugh's folks. They'd all be terribly hurt. So would our brothers and sisters—not to mention the families in our church. In fact, when I consider all the people I've nurtured spiritually over the years, I feel more than guilty. After all, my witness would sink drastically in their eyes. No telling the harm there!" She hesitated before mentioning,

131

THE TEMPTING OF AUDRA GREY

"Do you realize, Julie, if I were an immoral person, having a secret affair wouldn't hurt any of those people?"

Her friend laughed. "Yeah, but I know you, Audra Grey. Your conscience wouldn't allow you to do such a thing. And if you did, you'd be so miserable, you couldn't enjoy yourself."

Audra grinned. "You're right." Then she turned back to the ramifications of a divorce. "Hugh would still function OK, still plunk away contentedly at his computer. But I honestly think, although he wouldn't show it much, he'd hurt horribly. And I can't stand the thought of causing him that kind of grief."

Julie sighed. "And what about your grief, Audra? How much longer can you bear his treating you so shabbily? And how much more can you fight your feelings for Craig?"

"I can keep my life busy and full—"

"And totally joyless!" Julie cut in.

"Well, Jesus didn't promise us an easy road," Audra argued, then stopped herself. "What am I thinking about? I can't get a divorce. Not only would it hurt too many people and my witness, but it would hurt the Lord the most. And in my own heart, I'd always feel like an adulteress if I remarried."

Then she heard Julie meekly ask, "Are you saying I'm not free to remarry?"

"Your situation's different," Audra declared.

"Not that much."

They talked on until both women felt satisfied enough to say good night.

The next morning at work, Jeanette hailed Audra in the hall, surprising her with the question, "Do you plan to visit your parents in Hickory anytime soon?"

Audra smiled. "As a matter of fact, I had planned to ask Howard for a three-day weekend, because I haven't seen my folks since Andy's graduation. Why do you ask?"

"Well," Jeanette replied, waving some papers, "I can't really finish editing this manuscript until I check out a few things at the Biltmore Estate."

"Oh, yes! The Biltmore House. My family stopped there once on our way through Asheville. It's a spectacular place." Then

CHAPTER 20

Audra offered, "Would you like me to drop by and check out whatever questions you have?"

The other editor grinned mischievously. "I just happen to have those questions here. I could do the research by phone, I suppose, but it wouldn't be the same as getting the feel of those particular rooms." She handed Audra a short list. "Just be sure to keep the receipt for your tour ticket so the company will reimburse you."

"I'll remember." Audra folded the note and tucked it into her purse. Then she walked on to Howard's office, where she needed to take care of some important matters before she lost her nerve. Rapping gently, she slipped inside, then closed the door behind her.

The following weekend Audra journeyed toward her childhood home. Something inward drove her again to that nest where "Mama and Daddy" kissed away all hurts, where she could take refuge in the attic bedroom filled with memories. They would pull her back to a carefree time long before the disappointment with Hugh and the responsibility of bills—and the coming of Craig McGregor. Perhaps she would even duck behind the kitchen door, resurrect imaginary Jackie, and share her every woe.

Audra giggled at the preposterous thought. She, a grown woman, talking to a wall! In the next instant she sobered, realizing that she must make a final decision soon. She couldn't endure much longer being torn between Craig's allurement and her commitment to Hugh.

Audra crossed alone the mountainous border into North Carolina that Saturday morning. When the highway wandered through Asheville's hilly terrain a little later, she decided to postpone her visit to the Biltmore Estate until the return trip the next afternoon. For now her sights were set on Hickory and the hugs and love that awaited her there.

Hours later Audra was safely inside familiar white walls. Relaxing in air-conditioned comfort, she sipped at a tall lemonade and reveled in the banter of her loved ones. Their words enwrapped her as soothingly as the music of a slow movement of a symphony. "I wish I could stay for a month," she told them.

The next day, when she attended Sunday school and church

with her parents, long-time members recognized Audra and greeted her warmly.

The church sanctuary had been remodeled since she was a girl, but the sermons remained as old-fashioned as ever—the same kind of sermons that had taught her to appreciate God at a young age.

"And what would all these fine folks say if they knew the real Audra Grey?" she asked herself. What if they discovered how much she felt drawn to the mountains north of them because of a man who dwelled there—a man who was not her husband?

When Pastor Mooring stepped to the pulpit, his bushy white eyebrows twitched dramatically while he read 2 Peter 2:20 through 22, the text for his sermon:

> If after they have escaped the pollutions of the world through the knowledge of the Lord and Saviour Jesus Christ, they are again entangled therein, and overcome, the latter end is worse with them than the beginning. For it had been better for them not to have known the way of righteousness, than, after they have known it, to turn from the holy commandment delivered unto them. But it is happened unto them according to the true proverb, The dog is turned to his own vomit again; and the sow that was washed to her wallowing in the mire.

Audra cringed. Ugly words! But they fittingly described an ugly situation—that of returning to old sinful ways after truly dedicating oneself to the Lord. Audra wondered if she was dabbling too much in that gray area between clearly defined sin and a clear conscience. If she was, she could easily slip into the filth the proverb described. At the thought, an unladylike "yuck!" nearly escaped her.

The minister began to recount first the notorious tale of David and Bathsheba, then the story of Joseph and Potiphar's wife. He described the scenes so vividly that Audra felt as if she were watching them in Technicolor.

Concluding his sermon, Pastor Mooring asked, "And why did Joseph triumph over temptation whereas David slipped easily

CHAPTER 20

into sin? Here's the answer in just five words: Joseph fled, but David lingered."

The minister then appealed to his congregation not to toy with temptation, but to flee from it with the haste of a Joseph. "This is Mooring's own paraphrase of Proverbs 4:15," he boomed. "Don't look! Don't even consider! Just leave! Turn your back on it! Go!"

In moments the choir stood to sing the closing anthem. And as the music washed over her, Audra guessed that God may have just spoken again, this time through another clergyman. He was repeating, "Don't give up, Audra! You will make it through this valley."

Will I, Lord? "I feel too unworthy even to ask for Your help anymore," she prayed silently, then dabbed at some stray tears before her mother discovered them.

An hour later, when Audra left her parents' home and arrived at a crossroads, she faced the choice of turning either south toward Asheville or north toward Blowing Rock.

With Pastor Mooring's sermon still heavy upon her conscience, Audra turned the car south.

Chapter 21

Audra felt as if she had stepped suddenly into another time and place, to a castle, a chateau in the French countryside. But the ornate walls and windows and spired roofs towering above her belonged to the gentle slopes of Asheville, North Carolina.

Here, near the turn of the century, beneath the same serene gaze of Mount Pisgah and other lush-green peaks, George Washington Vanderbilt directed the construction of his Biltmore House.

To supplement Jeanette's research, Audra purchased a colorful booklet at a gift shop. The literature would tell the editor anything she needed to know about the Biltmore's 250 rooms, its art treasures and furnishings, as well as the gardens and vineyards beyond.

Despite the lightweight dress Audra wore, she felt smothered in a humid blanket. Tugging at the entrance door, she glanced at the black clouds clustering on the horizon. "The prelude to a good ol' Southern thunderstorm," she speculated.

"Welcome!" an attendant greeted her. "Here's a brochure for your self-guided tour," she said. "The way's well marked."

Plucking Jeanette's list from her purse, she walked directly over to the sunken, rounded room called the Winter Garden. Sunshine, pouring down from a domed skylight overhead glistened off the fountain and sculpture in the center. The bronze boy and geese didn't resemble a Greek warrior at all, she thought. Still, the statue spurred memories that took Audra back almost a year to her first walk with Craig McGregor. And

CHAPTER 21

the limestone archways encircling the room brought those memories into sharper focus.

Audra closed her eyes to shut out the recollections, but they wouldn't leave. "He even follows me here!" she thought in exasperation, then quickly jotted down some notes for Jeanette. "The steps and floor look like marble," she wrote, "and quite an array of palms and ferns and bright pink flowers decorate the room."

Marble. Craig once wished to sculpt me in marble.

In an effort to escape her thoughts, Audra rushed past the billiard room and on to the banquet hall, one of her favorite parts of the estate. Other visitors milled around inside, apparently as awestruck as she. The ceiling arched at least seventy feet above them, and the sheer scale of the chandeliers, the banquet table, and the triple fireplace was breathtaking in itself. Then came more statues and other works of art to gaze at—and sixteenth-century tapestries that told a story.

"A love story, no doubt!" Peering closer at the images of gods and goddesses gracing the walls, Audra smiled slyly. "It does, indeed, depict the proverbial triangle," she mused, "two men in love with one woman—or is the woman in love with both men?" Somehow Audra drew comfort from the realization that people living hundreds of years before grappled with the same moral issues she did. Solomon's saying, There is no new thing under the sun, still held true in her modern age.

She stopped at a Latin inscription which, translated, read, "Give us peace in our time, Lord."

Yes, that was her prayer too. But would the recent decisions she had made bring her that peace? Or would those decisions bring more upheaval, this time affecting Hugh and the children also?

Audra continued to brood as she wandered through cavernous halls and scribbled notes for Jeanette.

The final question dealt with Mr. Vanderbilt's own room. His canopy bed and other furnishings were scarlet with gold trim. Audra gazed beyond the Italian dressing table, beyond the parted draperies, at a stunning panorama of mountains, wooded vales, and fields of vivid green.

She lingered there, drinking in the natural beauty. In all his collecting of exquisite, man-made masterpieces, George

THE TEMPTING OF AUDRA GREY

Vanderbilt hadn't lost sight of the value of artwork that only God Himself could fashion. And there it dazzled through the windows, still enhancing the home long after Vanderbilt's time.

With the research for Jeanette completed, Audra was free to go. Instead, she took the stairs to the basement to visit again the bowling alley, indoor swimming pool, and gymnasium.

"Mr. Vanderbilt was certainly a grand host," she reflected, imagining how much fun it must have been to be invited there for a weekend.

In that moment John 14:2 came to mind: "In my Father's house are many mansions. . . . I go to prepare a place for you." "Jesus is the grandest host of all," she thought, "and He's preparing an even greater place than this for His followers." The idea took her breath away. The next moment, though, familiar woebegone feelings returned. "But will He consider me one of His followers when—"

The abrupt rush of muggy outdoor air cut off her question. She was distracted, too, by how the dark cloudbank had thickened and edged closer.

Back at her car, Audra decided to venture a little ways up the Blue Ridge Parkway and visit the Folk Art Center there. Whenever she had tried to convince Hugh to stop at the center, he was always too eager to reach his destination, whether heading east or west. Now, alone, Audra could play the part of sightseer.

Minutes later, she parked the car and strolled lazily up a path to the contemporary wooden-and-glass structure, so different from the turrets and spires she had just left.

Two elderly ladies under round-brimmed hats rested on benches nearby. A skinny man slouched beside them, his hands stuffed into faded jeans. His lanky legs and cowboy boots sprawled halfway across the walk.

"I'll tell ya," the skinny man was declaring in a thick Tennessean drawl, "that ol' mama cat was the best . . . catched mice . . . and had three litters of kittens right in a row."

When Audra reached the entrance, she overheard, "Them cats clumb up on top the car's engine—cut one of their tails clean off!"

Grimacing at the repulsive image his account inspired, Audra escaped through the door. Inside, the soothing strains of dulci-

CHAPTER 21

mer music floated throughout the open-beamed rooms. "Truly mountain!" she breathed. "A culture all its own."

Basking in the music, she strolled past book displays and postcards and on to the crafts. At every turn she saw Craig McGregor, in the handsculpted furniture and bowls; in the cutting boards of black walnut, oak, and cherry woods; and especially in the carvings that depicted southern Appalachian wildlife. There were swans, owls, rabbits, chipmunks, even geese in flight.

She remembered Christmastime at the airport, when a delicate wooden sparrow rested on Craig's open palm—his gift to her.

Such talent in those big, clumsy-looking hands! She saw again the sensitivity and openness in his expressive, pale eyes.

"Craig's not some devilish person, some wolf out for what he can get," she argued with herself. "He's warm and caring—and good." After all, he could easily have suggested some clandestine affair. Instead, he had proposed marriage—after a proper waiting spell, of course. And that hinged on Audra's decision—a decision she alone could make—whether to end legally her unhappy union with her husband.

Divorce. The word held no glamor. It did not fit with the commitments with God and with Hugh.

Standing there among other visitors, she came to a startling conclusion: "I must see him. I've got to share my decision with Craig—face to face."

Retracing her steps to the entrance and the dedication quilt displayed on the wall there, Audra pushed her way outside.

The Tennessean was just finishing his tale when she descended the cement stairs. "This fella hollers over to mah wife, 'Lady!' he sez, 'there's a smashed cat on yer tire!' Then all a sudden them other cats ridin' atop that engine jumped out and runned away. . . ."

Audra left the little group as the elderly ladies tittered politely and the skinny man announced, "Since then, ain't seen no moh cats 'round mah place!"

Audra climbed into her car and, with both anticipation and fear, guided the vehicle onto the Blue Ridge Parkway toward Blowing Rock—and Craig McGregor.

Chapter 22

The storm brewing behind Audra seemed to push her car up the road that snaked into the mountains. Already ash and maple trees were beginning to stir. Even the sky-blue chicory and black-eyed Susans tilted reluctantly, as if bracing themselves against the coming deluge.

Audra wondered about forces besides the wind that might be driving her eastward. The intense desire to see Craig, perhaps? And what unseen powers lurked behind that desire? The thought sent prickly shivers up her back.

She argued with her conscience, "But Craig's a part of my decision, so he deserves to know."

Considering the storm's threat, Audra admitted that the freeway back to Hickory, then the road north to Blowing Rock, would have been a more practical route. But she couldn't chance being spotted by some hometown friend who might mention it to her parents. And how would she ever explain her sudden reappearance? *Well, Mom, there's this big, sweet guy up on the Blue Ridge.*

In that moment Craig's bearded image returned to her, along with a surge of gratitude. Hadn't he offered her human warmth when her life had been nearly devoid of it? Hadn't he restored her self-worth when Hugh had made her feel unlovable? And hadn't Craig taught her to look again beyond her everyday tedium to the wonder and beauty of nature? He had helped her smile—even laugh.

Now here she was, heading toward this creative soul whose simple lifestyle she envied. At last she could see for herself his

CHAPTER 22

ridgetop home and the spectacular view he had so picturesquely described through the seasons.

She already saw hints of that view as her car climbed higher, staying just out of the storm's grasp. Thunder muttered behind her, and occasional arrows of lightning chased up the slopes.

"No wonder Craig loves living up here!" Audra sighed. It was like another world, far from the city's tension. Even the road bank was brightened with patches of clinging wildflowers. God hadn't forgotten a thing when He shaped these mountains, she mused.

Wanting to reach her destination before the storm hit, Audra increased pressure on the accelerator. Taking care to slow at the curves, she otherwise kept up the pace, racing against the fury at her back.

Wild azalea and rhododendron green bordered the road now. "Oh, to see those again when they're a wall of blossoms!" she breathed, remembering her youthful Sunday excursions along the Blue Ridge Parkway.

Audra's mind lingered on family, then reviewed the church service of that morning and the minister's sermon. Was she "returning to the mire" with this deliberate visit to Craig?

She would feel presumptuous asking God for strength against any temptation she might meet on McGregor's mountain. After all, she was going against the Bible's counsel by stepping deliberately into temptation's own territory.

"But I must see him, Lord—please!"

At clearings, Audra spotted ragged tongues of rain lapping at distant peaks and an ominous dark mist creeping over the woodsy hillsides nearer the parkway.

Finally an exit sign sent her down a ramp and toward Blowing Rock, past poplars and oaks and beside a scenic lake, where a stone wall rambled along the roadside.

Despite Craig's complaints about flatlanders taking over, Audra found some places forever the same, and this quaint town was one of them. Little on the main street had changed since her childhood. Perhaps some shops were called different names now, but they were the same stone-and-brick buildings.

She drove by the park with its servicemen's memorial that Craig had once alluded to. Further on, a bright yellow Victorian house, with dormers and gables galore, seemed to defy the dark sky hovering over it. Continuing, she drove between two old stone churches, more evidence of the Anglo-Saxon imprint left upon those mountains.

Audra then turned the car around and headed back to a small grocery, where the proprietor gave her directions to Craig's road. "It's best to go back onto the parkway," he suggested, "to the next exit up." Then he described the way in more detail. "The house sits almost right on the edge of the cliff. You can't miss it."

She practically yelled her "thank-you" to compete with a rumble of thunder before sprinting back to the car.

Spruce pine and cedar danced wildly along the way, and a tirade of thunder made Audra feel as if she had wandered into the thick of battlefield fire.

"Perhaps I have," she pondered, breathing deeply to slow her thudding heart.

Craig was standing on the porch when she pulled up the gravel lane to Grandpappy McGregor's cabin-made-new. Dressed in blue jeans and a plaid cotton shirt, half-buttoned with sleeves rolled up to his elbows, Craig laughed heartily. "Oh, ho! Welcome to Blowing Rock!"

He took Audra's hand and pulled her up the steps to the door, which was mostly glass. In fact, she noticed how that entire side of the house was largely composed of windows.

"And no wonder!" she thought, aware of the tremendous view, now blanketed under angry clouds.

Was she imagining things, or were the melancholy notes of a pan flute wafting through the house? "Must be his stereo system," she guessed.

Craig guided her to a small dining area, where a lone kerosene lamp burned atop a table of sturdy oak. Beyond it lay the living room. There a rock fireplace dominated one wall, while other walls of knotty pine glimmered in the faint lamplight. Then abruptly the room was illuminated when lightning flashed through the picture windows.

In that instant Audra could see beyond a beamed archway, where a large four-poster bed rested beneath a patchwork quilt.

CHAPTER 22

Craig's voice still held its welcoming tone. "You made it just in time to experience a storm right up here in the heavens where all the fussin' takes place."

She smiled at the familiar vernacular she had grown so fond of over the months. To think she had scoffed, calling it "hillbilly jargon" that first day!

"A mountain storm can be a fearsome thing, Miz—" He corrected himself. "A fearsome thing, Audra, but beautiful to watch. Because the electricity sometimes shuts down when it storms, I keep candles and kerosene handy." He glanced over at a cabinet in the living room. "And I'll have to unplug the stereo in a while, but not right yet. The storm's just at the barking stage now." Audra turned toward the window and watched nature's own fireworks light up the hillocks and coves below, then the distant mountainscape.

"It truly is beautiful!" she declared.

Evergreens beside the house made a soft roaring sound as the wind whipped at their branches. Audra nearly said aloud, "Like the sound of the surf," but held back the words. Memories would only make this time more difficult, she decided.

When Craig pulled out a chair for her, she settled into it across from him at the table.

The lamp's glow picked up reddish highlights in his beard as he asked, "So, tell me, beautiful lady—what brings you up this way?"

"Actually, I've come to say goodbye," she said softly.

The mirth drained instantly from his eyes, leaving only a haunting sadness. "My letter wasn't meant as a proposal," he defended himself, "just an assurance that I'd be in the running if you decided on a divorce."

The breathy notes of the pan flute continued to wrap around the wind's song and the drumming of thunder.

"Oh, Craig!" She shook her head slowly. "If I were ever free to marry again, you'd be my only choice. A woman would be crazy not to want a man like you. Sometimes I think you're a dream, not real. So much intelligence and imagination and gentleness all in one person! And I'm sure anyone living with you would never experience one boring moment."

THE TEMPTING OF AUDRA GREY

She then folded her hands on the table, pronouncing the words she had rehearsed again and again, "But I can't be that woman, Craig. A divorce would cause unfathomable hurt to my children and parents—even to Hugh. And I can't intentionally cause that kind of pain."

"But what about the pain your husband has inflicted over the years?"

A sad smile twisted at Audra's lips when she recalled an identical question from Julie. Quickly, she dismissed it with, "That's not relevant." Then she rushed on, "I'm a 'holder-upper,' remember? Consider the damage a divorce could do to my witness. So many lives would be affected by my fall."

"A divorce isn't a fall," he protested. "It's just the end of a legal contract."

"No, Craig. It would be the end of a sacred contract, and I can't be a party to that. I'd always wonder if the divorce were legal in the sight of God. And because of that doubt, I couldn't be truly happy married to you or any other man besides Hugh."

When she rose to her feet, Craig cocked his head questioningly. She drew a long breath, then continued, "A few weeks ago I gave my publishing company notice that I'm leaving. I've accepted a part-time teaching position at a college in Knoxville."

"Not on my account, I hope." There was a chill in his voice as Craig pushed aside his chair. Strolling over to the stereo, he pulled the plug. The wind was just beginning to hurl raindrops against the glass.

Audra followed him to the largest picture window and stood there, entranced by the spectacle. They were, indeed, "right up in the heavens where all the fussin' takes place."

"I'll admit you were a consideration in my decision to leave Nashville," she said. "But the biggest factor had to do with Hugh and me living apart. It's not right for a husband and wife to be separated so much."

"Hmmm! Does Hugh know about this yet?"

She giggled nervously. "Not exactly! And I'm not looking forward to telling him, either. Andy'll simply have to apply for grants, and my new job will help keep Natalie in college."

CHAPTER 22

There in the dimness, Audra saw that no smile returned to her, only the steady regard of Craig's somber eyes.

"And what about my book?" he asked.

"Howard will take over as your editor now," she informed him. "And I hope you'll send your newest manuscript to him when you finish it." The rain was coming harder, and Audra raised her voice to be heard. "You're the most talented man I've ever known, Craig, and I look forward to reading many more of your works."

Facing her, he clamped his giant hands on her shoulders. "I dread what you're about to say, Audra. You want to end your contact with me completely, don't you?"

She made a sound of exasperation and let her tears flow freely. "If I didn't care so much for you, I wouldn't have to do this," she cried. "But the only way I'll ever end the awful struggle inside me is to remove myself entirely from your influence."

"Even from my letters?"

"Especially from your letters."

His voice was barely audible above the storm. "But, Audra, I love you." Then, in the next moment, she felt his arms close around her. Leaning into Craig's strength, she sobbed against his chest. She could feel his fingertips gently stroking her hair.

"Stay here awhile," he coaxed. "At least wait out the storm. With this rain it's safe to build a fire on the hearth now."

She listened to his soft drawl washing over her, caressing her. She felt so comfortable—at peace—in his arms.

Then suddenly lightning flashed again and illuminated the bed, much closer now. And in that one fleeting moment, Audra pictured herself lying there next to Craig with firelight flickering close by, mingling with the same soothing sounds of rain.

Joseph fled, but David lingered.

"No!" She pushed away from him. "Please, forgive me for hurting you. I should have had the sense and courage to give your manuscript over to another editor long ago when I first noticed the attraction between us," she said. "I think that would have spared us both a lot of grief."

But then you never would have rediscovered your worth as a woman, the beauty all around you, or the value in little things.

Her head was spinning, fighting the urge to forget propriety, to desert her responsibilities, her faith, the stuff that Audra Grey was made of. She could so easily meld into this mountain man's world. The idea was alluring, intoxicating.

"But I can't betray my Jesus," her voice trembled.

Gazing one last time into the pale eyes, Audra noticed a trace of compassion there. "Goodbye, Craig McGregor!" she said, then rushed out the door into the darkness.

After the car choked to a reluctant start, Audra backed it down the drive, then turned onto the gravelly road toward the parkway.

Lightning continued to scorch the night, followed by deafening peals of thunder. The little car quaked as it timidly nosed between tossing trees. While the windshield wipers clacked futilely against the storm, Audra squinted at the rain that swept across the road in blinding sheets.

She felt as if she were drowning, not in the waters lashing against the car, but in a deep loneliness, in grief, in a terror about the future. It stretched ominously before her like an empty, trackless wasteland. There would be no more letters to boost her morale, no more soft, deep voice over the phone, no more blue-eyed glances brimming with admiration.

Abruptly she was startled back to reality and the roadway. "I can't see!" Should she dare stop right where she was?

Another flash of lightning revealed something large looming ahead. An overpass. She inched toward it, then pulled off the road and hid under the archway of sturdy gray stones.

Bowing her head on the steering wheel, Audra wept uncontrollably, wrenching sobs that, after a time, left her exhausted. Then she lifted her face and noticed something odd. The thunder still rolled, the wind still blew as fiercely as before, and the rain continued its torrent. But there in her niche under the stone overpass, the storm seemed muffled, less threatening—almost peaceful. And flitting through her mind were the words of an old hymn:

He hideth my soul in the cleft of the rock . . .
And covers me there with His hand.

CHAPTER 22

Audra felt as if God were nudging her again, reminding her of His constant care. Life's storms might rage ahead of her, behind, and all around. But in His niche she could always find safety.

It was true that she couldn't depend upon Craig for nurturing anymore. But then neither should she depend upon Hugh, her children, Julie, even herself or her work—only upon God.

She repeated one of her favorite verses from Psalms, "He shall cover thee with his feathers, and under his wings shalt thou trust."

"Lord," she breathed, "I do trust You in this moment. I feel Your presence, Your protection, the intimacy I've craved for so long." But then her thoughts leaped ahead. What would happen when the psychological storms hit her—when Hugh coldly turned her away—would she be able to trust God then?

She paraphrased what a centurion had uttered nearly two thousand years before, "I trust, Lord. Help my untrust."

When the wind began to die and the rain pattered gently upon the laurel, Audra put her car in gear and headed down the dark parkway toward home.

Chapter 23

Despite Hugh's predictions of doom, when Audra moved back to Knoxville the sun still rose each morning and set each evening. Andy went on to medical school, and his sister remained in college, eventually graduating with honors.

Shortly thereafter Natalie married a young accountant much like her father, but more outgoing than Hugh. To Audra's delight, her son-in-law lavished his bride with affection, and the newlyweds enjoyed the kind of communication the mother had always longed for.

Several cycles of seasons had to pass before Audra could untangle herself from a web of memories. Autumn brought with it a mental tapestry of Appalachian sassafras and tulip poplars in the calico colors Craig had once described. Then, as chilled months waned and Audra grew impatient for trees to leaf again, her thoughts would drift back to her longest, most trying winter. With the earth's warming, she occasionally recalled the poetic lines of Craig's first book:

When Eddie Mae was seven and I was nearing twelve, mountain laurel suddenly burst into blushing bloom . . .

And her mind would stray again to the Blue Ridge with its "thickety bresh" looking all decked out in lacy pink pinafores.

One spring morning, when the memories unexpectedly returned, blotting out the sunshine like dark draperies, the doorbell chimed. There on the front porch stood tall, blond Marsha Maynard.

CHAPTER 23

"Hello!" she trilled. "I'm here to help plan the church's annual women's retreat."

"Oh, yes!" Audra replied absent-mindedly, inviting her inside. "Where are your little girls?"

"With their grandmother at the mall, searching for new Easter outfits."

"Lucky them!"

"Lucky me!"

Audra chuckled as she led her guest to the kitchen. The two women had served on several of the same church committees and had taught in Vacation Bible School together. But with their respective busy lives, they had never grown close. "Would you care for a cup of tea?" Audra asked.

"No, thank you!" Marsha dropped a notebook and other papers on the table. "I promised Mom I'd meet her at noon, so, if you don't mind, I'd like to get started."

"Sure!" Audra pulled up a chair while glancing at the papers in front of her. "Is this the schedule from last year?"

"Yes." The visitor handed her a list. "I've found several speakers who would be willing to come in October, but this one gives a terrific seminar on the four temperaments."

Suddenly the blond head stopped bobbing and concentrated on Audra. "Don't tell me—let me guess your personality traits!" Marsha's green eyes sparkled as she considered aloud. "With your love of lists and literature and your organizational skills, I'd say you're a melancholy/choleric."

"You're right." Audra grinned. "And with your yen for social events and your list making too, I'd suppose you're a sanguine/melancholy."

"Almost," Marsha admitted. "The melancholy is stronger. Its perfectionism keeps the undisciplined ways of the sanguine under control." Then she asked, "Has Hugh ever been tested? He's a real puzzle to me."

Audra burst into laughter. "He's been a puzzle to me for years. But, yes, at several seminars we discovered he's a phlegmatic/choleric."

"That's impossible," Marsha retorted.

"What do you mean?"

THE TEMPTING OF AUDRA GREY

"God would never create a person with two such opposing temperaments as the easygoing phlegmatic and the hard-driving choleric. Hugh must have fibbed on the test."

Audra shrugged. "Well, then he fibbed all three times. I doubt if anyone could pull that off, not even someone as intelligent as my husband."

"Hmmm!" Marsha had pushed the stack of papers aside, obviously distracted by the mystery enshrouding Hugh's personality. "Then I think there's only one other explanation."

"What's that?"

"One of Hugh's temperaments is phony. It must have been forced on him as a child."

"Are you serious?" Audra exclaimed, intrigued now at the visitor's psychoanalysis of her husband.

"Quite! Tell me, is either of his parents so domineering that he might have been forced to play the phlegmatic role?"

Audra pondered the question before answering, "Not that domineering. They're farmers, you know. Everyone's too caught up in work."

"Ah ha! That's it. I'd bet your husband was born a phlegmatic/sanguine, whose easygoing, fun-loving nature was squelched before it ever got the chance to develop. With all that farmwork to do, his parents turned the sanguine part of him into a choleric." Marsha clicked her tongue sympathetically. "Poor Hugh! He must be miserable most of the time."

"I wouldn't know," Audra said. "Hugh isn't one to share his feelings."

"Neither was Dave, until we started counseling a few months ago."

Surprised, Audra asked, "You and Dave are seeing a marriage counselor?"

Marsha nodded sadly. "Let's forget the retreat for now, huh? I feel like talking instead."

Audra could sense her choleric temperament rebelling against the suggestion, but she conceded. "All right! Let's go into the living room, where it's more comfortable."

The two women sank down on the couch. Curling her stockinged feet under her, Audra faced the visitor. "May I ask why you and Dave decided upon counseling?"

CHAPTER 23

"My husband had an affair," Marsha blurted. With tears clouding her eyes, she continued, "It was only a one-time incident, but Dave felt so guilty that he came straight home and asked my forgiveness."

"I'm so sorry! You must have been devastated."

Marsha uttered a short whimpering sound. "I can't begin to describe all the feelings I experienced that awful night. The worst was betrayal. I felt Dave had betrayed not only me, but our daughters, his parents, my parents—"

"Your dog, your parakeet!" Audra teased, happily noting the resultant lopsided grin on her friend's face. "Seriously, though, how are things between you and Dave now?"

"To tell the truth, I think our relationship is better than it's ever been—and so is our spiritual life." A self-conscious giggle escaped Marsha's lips. "I wish we had started our first months of marriage with the intense counseling we've received over the last several months. Then, perhaps, we wouldn't have slid into such harmful habits—habits that chipped away at our relationship."

When Audra's eyebrows raised inquisitively, Marsha explained. "Dave and I never really developed the keen communication skills we're learning now. We had become so busy with working and raising our girls, even with church activities, that interaction between us seemed to keep getting shoved aside. We hardly ever did anything fun together anymore. It's no wonder Dave was so attracted—however briefly—to that other woman."

Audra nodded, understanding more than her visitor could realize.

"Our counselor has helped us reestablish our family worship times. My husband and I actually go out on a date once a week now. And we write love notes to each other." She beamed. "He's even brought me flowers!"

Now Audra's eyes were the ones filling with tears. "I'm truly happy for you," she said. "I wish Hugh would agree to counseling, but—" She stopped midsentence and considered her next words. Long ago Julie had suggested Audra open up to someone in her church, but could Marsha be trusted with such a personal disclosure?

Slowly, cautiously, Audra unraveled the truth about her and

THE TEMPTING OF AUDRA GREY

Hugh's marriage. And as she grew more comfortable in Marsha's presence, she even revealed a little about the "other man" who had wanted a place in her life.

When Audra finished, her friend remained silent a few moments. Then Marsha said, "As I mentioned earlier, Hugh is a big puzzle. I can easily understand why you felt so starved emotionally. And I feel ashamed for not reaching out to you and offering some support."

"But you didn't know." Audra shook her head. "No one knew, not even my own parents. I kept everything a secret—except the few times I phoned Julie or when I spoke to a counselor."

Marsha perked up. "So you did attempt counseling?"

"Oh, yes! And Hugh came—once. But he said it was a waste of money, because he didn't plan to make any effort toward change."

Frowning, Marsha said, "Sometimes, with a man like Hugh, it takes something earth-shattering to open his eyes. That's sad."

"Yes, it is," Audra murmured, her downturned mouth suddenly switching to a radiant smile. "I want you to know, Marsha, how much I appreciate your allowing me to share the truth with you today. Sometimes I feel so powerless that I even avoid visiting my folks alone for fear I'll take a detour and head for Craig's place instead."

"We're all powerless in our own strength," Marsha pointed out. "We can only rely on a greater power than what we have ourselves. I'm sure you realize that's the Holy Spirit's job."

Audra sighed. "Yes, but it's awfully hard for a choleric like me to admit my weakness."

Sympathy flowed through Marsha's voice. "Listen! When you need to unload to someone, just phone me day or night. I'm never too busy for a friend."

Friend? "What a beautiful word!" Audra reflected. Had the Lord finally sent her a true friend, someone to take Julie's place there in Knoxville?

Her answer came when Marsha suggested they end their time together on their knees in prayer.

Chapter 24

Audra's newfound friendship with Marsha and her love for college teaching helped loosen memory's hold on her heart. But an even greater love gradually pushed the intruding image of Craig McGregor aside until he became a warm blur in a corner of her mind.

That greater love was Bryan, Audra's first grandchild. He filled her empty arms with new joy as her old nurturing instincts rushed to the aid of the squirmy creature whose every smile became her own.

Hugh also delighted in caring for the little fellow. And as Bryan grew, so did Audra's hopes again whenever she watched her husband cuddling and rocking the boy. She thought that surely this man, who tenderly stroked tiny curls and whispered nonsensical phrases into a pink ear, could learn to do similar things for her, his wife.

Two years later, however, Audra still waited for that change in her husband. She reminded herself frequently that her happiness didn't hinge on Hugh anymore or upon other people or things—only upon her relationship with God. "And that's been great," she mused every time she thought about it.

As if testing her commitment, catastrophe struck her husband's business one dazzling August day. A group of three doctors plus two other clients decided to abandon the accounting firm and go with another, leaving Hugh in shock and despair.

As soon as the news reached Natalie, she drove across town, bringing Bryan in an effort to cheer her father.

THE TEMPTING OF AUDRA GREY

"He still looks gloomy to me," the young mother commented later.

Audra agreed with a slight nod. She and Natalie were stretched out on lawn chairs, watching Hugh and the toddler play in the shade of the chestnut trees down the slope. The day was mild, everything looking mellow in the golden sunlight.

Lazily, Audra stirred. "Your father didn't need so many clients," she insisted. "It's time he slowed down a bit and enjoyed life for a change."

"Ha!" Natalie scoffed. "Dad'll never slow down, and you know it. He'll probably find even more clients than the ones he's lost. We're all workaholics in this family," she decreed.

"Not so!" Audra said. "I'm a *reformed* workaholic. You'll note I work only two days a week now. I've learned to schedule timeouts for myself, and sometimes I toss my to-do list in the trash and spend an entire day tramping around in the hills or visiting friends—in other words, doing absolutely nothing constructive at all."

Natalie giggled. "I'm impressed. And I've noticed you don't hold as many offices in the church anymore, either."

"Oh, I've kept my Sunday school class, and I still sing in the choir and things," her mother said. "But you're right. I was spreading myself too thin and was fast getting frazzled." She grinned at her daughter, feigning an ancient voice. "Anyway, it's time for you younger folks to begin taking over for us old codgers."

Natalie laughed. "I already have." Then she sobered. "Truthfully, Mom, what about Dad? Is he going to get through this trouble all right? I've never seen him so discouraged."

Audra looked again at Hugh, who was methodically playing horsey, jostling Bryan on his knee. "Neither have I," she confided. "I wish he could learn to relax. We don't need much money anymore. The house and cars are paid for; Andy's almost on his own and will set up a practice eventually."

Natalie made a purring sound. "Andy and Michelle, you mean!"

"Yes—Michelle," Audra replied, picturing the dark-eyed beauty who had captured her son's heart and would soon become his wife.

CHAPTER 24

Natalie roused herself from the chair, half-groaning, "Well, I guess I'd better pry my son away from his grandpa and get on home. I still have supper to fix."

"Uh-huh," Audra murmured. "Please forgive me, dear, for not budging, but I think I'm turning into a human sloth."

"That's OK, Mom."

Audra listened to her daughter's fading footfalls, then drowsed in the sunshine's buttery warmth.

Moments later a child's wailing abruptly brought her mind into sharp focus. Bryan sprawled on the ground, crying. . . . Natalie's eyes bulged with fright and her soundless mouth gaped. . . . Hugh, clutching his chest, was crumpling into a heap on the grass. The scene looked strange, as if everyone were moving in slow motion.

Audra was quickly at her husband's side. "Natalie, call an ambulance!" she ordered, while struggling to turn Hugh over. Then she gasped, stricken by the sight of his ashen face. Instinctively she tilted his head back to clear the airway and bent to his mouth. No breath. His chest was as still as the ground beneath him. Her trembling fingers groped for his neck and the carotid pulse. *Please, be beating!* Nothing.

With both hands she ripped open Hugh's shirt and pressed her ear against his clammy flesh. Again, nothing.

Feeling for the lower tip of the breastbone, she measured two finger-widths up, clasped her hands over the spot, then locking her elbows, pushed down with all her might. "One-and-two-and . . ." *Don't you dare die on me, Hugh Grey!* "Six-and-seven-and-eight-and . . ." *You haven't learned to live yet.* "Fourteen-and-fifteen!" She blew two quick breaths into her husband's mouth. Again, "One-and-two-and . . ."

How long she knelt there—working over him, praying, weeping, scolding Hugh for bringing this upon himself—she didn't know. Time became a muddle of counting . . . breathing . . . even a battle with profound dizziness. There were unfamiliar forms and voices. Then Natalie clutched her, crying, "Mom! Mom!"

"Mom? Are you asleep?"

Audra's eyes fluttered open and stared at the inquisitive faces of Natalie and Bryan overhead. "Your father?" she asked anxiously.

155

THE TEMPTING OF AUDRA GREY

"Oh, he's still down there moping," Natalie said.

Bolting upright, Audra's gaze fell upon the sagging figure of her husband. With uncontained joy, she nearly shouted, "He's all right!"

"What?"

"Excuse me, sweetheart! But I've got a husband to hug." Audra pecked her daughter on the cheek, dismissing her with, "I'll see you both tomorrow!" Then she flew down the slope to the white wrought-iron love seat that rested between the chestnuts. There Hugh slouched, looking as pensive as ever.

"I just had the most horrible dream," she said lightly, dropping down beside him.

He glanced over at her in dismay as if to ask, "So why do you seem so delighted about it?"

Audra rushed clumsily ahead, afraid to measure her words, afraid that any serious thought about them might squelch her resolve. This was her husband's "road to Damascus" experience. He was vulnerable now, perhaps willing to listen.

"Hugh, I dreamed you had a heart attack right here in our yard, that you had literally worked yourself into an early grave." Her voice quivered, and tears began to sting at her eyes. "I tried desperately to revive you, but you just lay there and wouldn't breathe. The whole hideous scene was so real—it really shook me up!"

Hugh regarded her solemnly a moment, then chided, "Don't be so melodramatic, Audra! It was just a dream."

"But dreams sometimes reveal our deepest fears, honey." She took his hand in hers and squeezed it gently. "Tell me, do you plan to replace all five of the clients you've lost?"

Hugh looked incredulous. "Of course! And maybe I can pick up a few smaller—"

With ire mounting, Audra raised her hand to his lips and stopped the words. "Hugh Grey, you listen to me! There are other things in life besides work. You need to take more time out for yourself, for God, for friends, for *us*!"

"Yes?" The word mocked her. "Then who's going to keep up our property taxes, and who's going to help Andy get established, and who will help fund the repaving of our church parking lot?"

CHAPTER 24

Audra persisted, "I think you should replace only one or two clients. With my job, we will have enough to pay taxes and other bills. Andy's a big boy now," she reminded her husband. "He's quite capable of establishing a practice without our help. As for the church parking lot, give other members a chance to be generous!"

"That's irresponsible," Hugh said.

His wife stared unseeingly at the road below them. "You don't get it, do you?" she huffed. "You don't even recognize your need to start experiencing the life you've kept buried beneath work for so many years. Will you ever slow down enough to enjoy these flowers we've planted or to travel a little, maybe just sit out here with me and marvel at a few sunsets? I want us to have some fun together, Hugh, before—" she stammered, "before something like my dream really does happen."

Frowning, Hugh declared, "A man can't shirk his responsibilities, Audra." Then he launched into a lengthy monologue as if trying to justify to himself the compelling need to continue his workaholic lifestyle.

Ordinarily, because Audra disdained confrontation, she would have given in to him. But today was different. Today she had dreamed of Hugh's lifeless body on the grass. The horror of that dream fed her courage, and long-repressed feelings came spewing forth. "Hugh, we've done it. Our kids have turned into good Christian adults, able to manage their own lives now. We have the right to slow down."

"As I said, I don't agree—"

She cut him off. "Do you have any idea how your obsession for fulfilling your responsibility nearly drove me away?" Her breath caught in her throat. *Should I tell him?*

Hugh shrugged in icy silence.

"Do you remember long ago when I asked your opinion about corresponding with a male writer-friend?"

"Uh-hum."

Inhaling deeply, Audra began telling her husband about her relationship with Craig McGregor, how it had started in downtown Nashville, about Christmastime at the airport, the ensuing letters, the writers' conference, Mount Rainier, the coast, and even about their adjoining rooms and the almost overwhelming temptation she faced that rainy night.

Audra paused, trying to assess her husband's reaction. But, as usual, Hugh's stony face didn't even hint at his feelings.

New tears coursed down her cheeks when she reminded him of their futile attempt at counseling. "I begged you," she sobbed. "I needed you to love me, but you seemed set upon driving me to the arms of another man."

She then tried to convey her own moral struggle throughout those long months. "I didn't want to forsake you or the Lord," she said, "but you didn't seem to care. Phone calls were too expensive, you argued." On and on she talked until she concluded, "I've learned to live without your affection, Hugh. Only God provides my nurturing now. He's my strength." Then in a small voice she admitted, "But if you ever should decide to show your love to me, I wouldn't mind."

Having averted her eyes, Audra gathered the nerve to peer again into her husband's face and was stunned by what she found there. Plainly shaken, Hugh stared at her. And was that a glint of tears she saw?

A new tone gentled his voice when he asked, "Don't you realize you're the only woman I've ever loved?"

"I am?" *But how do you expect me to know that?*

To Audra's surprise, he slipped his arm around her and pulled her head against his chest. "I've tried to show that love by the things I do," he explained, "by providing a good home and other material things." Hugh suddenly looked embarrassed. "I'm not a good talker like you or that McGregor fellow. I could never come up with such fancy words."

"The phrase 'I love you' isn't so hard," she offered, "just three syllables. I'd be quite contented hearing that from you just once a day."

"I don't know, Audra. I'm pretty set in my ways. I'd need help." Then a wan smile lifted the grim corners of his mouth. "Do you suppose Dr. Kelchner still has a practice in this town?"

"He might," she said calmly, but her head was in a whirl. "Are you agreeing to counseling?" she asked.

"Audra, I'd die if I lost you," her husband said. "I want to make

CHAPTER 24

you happy, but truthfully, I don't know how. Maybe Dr. Kelchner can teach me...."

Audra glanced up at Hugh's earnest face. She could feel her senses spinning and soaring. Was this real or another dream?

Her eyes darted heavenward. *Thank You, Lord*! Then she focused on the hills crouching in the distance, beyond which rose the Great Smoky Mountains, miles away. Her mind meandered over those peaks to the Blue Ridge beyond, where a certain cabin rested on a clifftop.

And thank you, Craig McGregor!